GUIDE TO THE LONGBOW

Brian Sorrells

STACKPOLE BOOKS

Copyright © 2014 by Stackpole Books

Published by
STACKPOLE BOOKS
5067 Ritter Road
Mechanicsburg, PA 17055
www.stackpolebooks.com

Printed in China

10 9 8 7 6 5 4 3 2 1

FIRST EDITION

Cover design by Tessa J. Sweigert

Library of Congress Cataloging-in-Publication Data

Sorrells, Brian J.
  Guide to the longbow : [tips, advice, and history for target shooting and hunting] / Brian Sorrells. — First edition.
      pages cm
  Includes index.
  ISBN 978-0-8117-1458-7
1. Archery. 2. Longbows. 3. Bowhunting. I. Title.
  GV1185.S595 2014
  799.3'2—dc23
                          2014010397

Contents

ACKNOWLEDGMENTS

This book is dedicated, as always, to my beautiful daughters, Rachel and Claire Sorrells. You two are the pride of my life and a never-ending source of strength and inspiration. You have both been candles in the window for me on many a dark and stormy night. I'm proud of you and love you beyond words.

I also wish to thank T. J. Conrads and Don Thomas, whose support and kindly criticism over the years have improved my writing immeasurably, and whose faith in my ability has allowed me many more chances to be published than I probably deserved.

Thanks also to Mitch Crawford, a close friend from my days in the military, with whom I've shared many a wild adventure; and to The Meat Hogs, with whom I had the distinct pleasure of sharing a "grunt hunt" in Tennessee a few years back.

Thanks to all of my fellow outdoorsmen who "do it right." Someone once said that a person's morals are measured by what he or she does when no one is looking.

And finally, thanks to Byron Padgett, a fellow police officer, photographer, and outdoor writer who has really been there and done that, and whose comedy and company I enjoy while chasing deer and turkeys on "the farm." As long as Jodi continues to let us hunt together, that is . . .

FOREWORD

Scores of enthusiastic archers have produced countless volumes of fact and fiction in an attempt to capture the feeling of watching a swiftly flying arrow and the satisfaction of seeing it strike the target. Inside every bent stick there is a bow, and in the wake of every arrow's passing there lies a story.

The longbow is my chosen instrument. To me, a fine longbow is the equivalent of a blues guitarist's Fender Stratocaster. While recurve bows are equally beautiful and efficient, it is the longbow—and those who hunt with them—that I hope to honor with this book. Being a longbowman is as much a state of mind as a way of life, and the term brings to my mind pictures of legendary archers like Howard Hill, Saxton Pope, and Arthur Young, or Will and Maurice Thompson. For them, the longbow was a conduit to another world, one free from the cares of society. The longbow provided adventure, food, and lasting friendships.

The wilds of their times are mostly gone, but we modern longbowmen (and women) still crave wild game taken with the longbow and arrow, and the fields, forests, and mountains where that game lives. I envision the modern longbowman much as I do the mountain man of the Old West—silhouetted against the rising sun, clad not in buckskin and moccasins but in dark, soft clothing and boots, with a well-worn back quiver sprouting arrows fletched with barred turkey feathers, and a longbow resting easily across one shoulder as he searches the deep purple valley for signs of his quarry.

- 1 -

History of the Longbow

Like many other tools used today, no one knows for sure exactly when, where, or how the first longbow or arrow was created. While carbon dating gives scientists an idea of how old archaeological artifacts are, many unanswered questions still remain. It's unlikely that the bow and arrow, used by so many cultures, originated in a single region and spread around the globe. Instead, they were probably discovered in many separate cultures and geographic areas, resulting in variations in construction and development. A good example is the contrast between the wood bows made by Native Americans here on our continent and the composite horn bows made by the Turks. There are even notable differences among Native American bows and arrows, since tribes used whatever material was on hand to make them. The Plains Indians used hardwoods like hickory because these trees were abundant where they lived and the wood was strong enough to make the shorter bows needed to hunt and shoot from horseback. The Cherokee preferred Osage orange (also known as hedge apple); a bow made from this wood lasted for years and seldom broke. Material for arrows included river cane, witch hazel, and dogwood shoots.

Many archery relics have been discovered that give us an idea of how long the bow and arrow have been in use in different areas of the world. For instance, stone arrowheads were discovered in Africa dating to 25,000 BC, and archaeologists believe that bows may have been used there as far back as 40,000 BC. A couple of Neolithic (10,000 BC–2000 BC) bows were found in Europe—one in Somerset, England, and the other near the town of Rotten Bottom, Scotland. The Scottish bow, made of yew, was carbon-dated to about 3800 BC.

The discovery of King Henry VIII's ship *Mary Rose*, which sank at Portsmouth, England, in 1545, revealed that the ship was carrying 137 intact longbows and 3,500 arrows. Many of these artifacts were recovered, and several were in good enough condition to test. The average draw weight of these bows was 100 pounds. Considering they had been submerged in silt for such a long period of time, it's safe to say that in new condition their draw weights would have been much more.

These longbows ranged in length from 6 feet 2 inches to 6 feet 11 inches, with the average length being 6 feet 6 inches. The arrows were usually 24 to 32 inches long, with an average length of 30 inches, and were made of beech, ash, poplar, and hazel. These shorter lengths made little difference since the English bowman drew the arrow to his chest, which required less arrow length than the standard method of drawing and shooting longbows today.

Since the United States and England share such close ties, it's important to look at the development of the longbow in both countries. Many battles were fought in England before the introduction of firearms, and in several of these engagements the powerful longbow in the hands of trained archers was the deciding factor in the fight's outcome. Accounts of these battles make fascinating reading for those interested in an in-depth history of the longbow.

THE LONGBOW IN ENGLAND

Probably the most famous longbowman from the archery era—and the one whom most people equate with that period—was Robin Hood, who was said to steal from the rich and give to the poor. There are so many different descriptions of Robin Hood that it's impossible to draw any definite conclusions as to his actual stature. Some report him as being a mere "bag of bones," while others claim he was a giant man with a bow of such strength that no other man could shoot it. His feats with the longbow also drew a great deal of skepticism, as he was reported to have shot an arrow a mile and to have slain one of the king's deer at 300 yards.

Another legendary figure, William Tell, was allegedly a traveling teller of stories and intricate tales. In 1307 AD, he refused to bow to a hat mounted on a pole, a sign of imperial authority, and was ordered to shoot an apple off his son's head as punishment. Legend tells us that William Tell was successful in the attempt.

While there are no actual historical records of these feats, one can't help but believe that these stories are part of the allure of the longbow, and that many modern longbow shooters have tried to copy Robin Hood's trick of splitting an arrow at a hundred paces. That's why when an archer manages to shoot an arrow (whether intentionally or accidentally) with enough accuracy to split another arrow already in the target, he or she refers to this feat as a "Robin Hood."

History does tell us that during the Anglo-Norman invasion of Wales, which occurred slowly from 1066 to about 1109, the Welsh bowmen took such a heavy toll on the invaders that the English army was quick to note how effective the longbow was as a weapon of war. After their victory, the English immediately began incorporating Welsh bowmen conscripts into their own army. From then on, the longbow became a very important part of English culture.

During the Crusades (circa 1095–1291), English knights and their longbows were pitted against the Mohammedan army, whose soldiers used mainly crossbows.

Recognizing that the longbow required much practice to master, King Edward I (1272–1307) wanted to be sure that there was always a ready supply of archers on hand and passed an edict banning all sports on Sundays except for archery. Every male was required to practice archery, and those who did not were said to have faced dire consequences. Archers were required to build up their strength until they could draw a bow between 160 and 180 pounds in draw weight. Skeletons of longbow archers from that era show deformations, with enlarged left arms and bone spurs on the left shoulders, left wrists, and right fingers.

The legendary Battle of Northallerton on August 22, 1138, demonstrated that the English had readily adopted the longbow as a weapon of war. With each English archer capable of firing ten arrows a minute accurately out to a range of more than 200 yards, the longbowmen used a hail of arrows to keep the invading Scotsmen from advancing.

The majority of English bows were made of English yew (*Taxus baccata*). England had been importing yew for bows since 1294, and in 1492 began demanding a "docking fee" of four yew bow staves per every ton of cargo brought into an English port. In 1350, Henry IV began sending his bow makers onto private property to secure yew trees. As the availability of yew lessened because of such high demand, bowyers started using other woods such as ash, elm, or hazel.

Bowstrings were made from flax, hemp, or silk. It was said that on rainy days bowmen would carry their bowstrings under their helmets to keep them dry. Arrows were usually fletched with goose feathers, though other types would be used if necessary. They were typically fletched with a bodkin point (a sort of field point with square shoulders) or a barbed broadhead-type point. These points, driven by the powerful force of the longbow, were highly effective, even against chainmail.

Gerald of Wales commented on the efficiency of the longbow in the twelfth century, recounting an incident in which a soldier on horseback was struck by an arrow shot at him by a Welshman. The arrow went through his thigh despite his iron armor, continued through the skirt of his leather tunic, penetrated the saddle, and finally entered the horse far enough to kill it.

The longbow featured prominently in some of the most well-known battles of the Hundred Year's War (1337–1453) between the English and French, including the Battles of Crecy and Agincourt. The Battle of Crecy took place on August 26, 1346, when Edward III led his army against the French. It was a success for the English longbowmen, with approximately fifteen hundred Frenchmen killed and only fifty English soldiers lost.

The Battle of Agincourt on October 25, 1415, demonstrated new English battle tactics. Longbow archers in past wars were usually protected from oncoming cavalry by pits strategically dug to slow down opposing forces on horseback. However, at Agincourt the English used sharpened stakes embedded in the ground facing the enemy. The rushing cavalry troops were forced to split their ranks to go around these obstacles, which made them easier to defeat.

Historians believe that there were approximately 5,000 English archers at the Battle of Agincourt, and that each archer likely carried around 100 arrows. If these archers were truly capable of firing 10 arrows a minute, the French would have advanced under a hail of about 500,000 arrows!

English archers were less successful after these battles. Their lines broke at the Battle of Verneuil in 1424, then were completely routed at the Battle of Patay in 1429. Changes in battle tactics likely led to these defeats, as the French would surely have studied the standard English formations and figured out a way to circumvent the deadly hail of arrows.

In the mid-1500s, the musket began to replace the longbow as a weapon of war. By 1595, all longbows in the English army were ordered to be replaced by muskets.

THE LONGBOW IN NORTH AMERICA

There is a little-known legend that tells of a man who landed in the New World more than three hundred years before Columbus's voyage in 1492. A Welsh prince named Madog ab Owain Gwynedd, also known as Madoc, sailed from home in order to avoid violence there. The legend says that Madoc and his companions settled and intermarried with Native Americans, possibly somewhere in the area of what is now Kentucky. On November 26, 1608, a member of an exploration party entered the villages of the Eastern Siouan Monacan Indians above the falls of the James River in Virginia. He reported that some of the natives spoke a language resembling Welsh. While this is only a legend and there is little scientific proof that it actually occurred, it's interesting to think that maybe Madoc introduced his knowledge of the longbow to Native Americans in the area.

We do know that prior to the colonization of the New World by the white man, Native Americans lived by the bow and arrow. However, the development of the modern longbow in America would not come about until much later, in the early twentieth century, with a Native American named Ishi.

In 1911, on the outskirts of a small California town called Oroville, a naked and half-starved man was discovered in a corral at the edge of town. The sheriff, not knowing what to do with the man, who spoke no English, did the only thing he could think of—he provided him with food and clothing and housed the poor man in the local jail. Even though Ishi had committed no crime, the sheriff thought it best to protect him from curious eyes. Many "experts" in Native American languages were brought in but none of them could speak the man's strange dialect. Finally, a professor from the University of California visited and happened upon a word that Ishi understood. The professor discovered that Ishi was a member of the Yana tribe, believed to be extinct. They nearly were—Ishi was the last surviving member of the tribe. The professor brought Ishi back to the university to study him, and soon Ishi made friends with a physician there named Saxton Pope. Pope had an interest in archery, and Ishi showed him how he made bows, arrows, and arrow points. The two, along with Pope's friend and fellow archery enthusiast Arthur Young, spent much time learning from each other.

Ishi died of tuberculosis in 1916, but Pope and Young's interest in the longbow only grew. They experimented with different bow designs and eventually decided that the English style of longbow was much more efficient than any Indian style. They stuck with the English style for the remainder of their hunting careers. They also tried different types of wood before deciding that the best was one that any medieval archer would have easily recognized—yew.

Pope and Young had many adventures with the bow and arrow, some of which are recorded in Pope's book, *Hunting with the Bow and Arrow*. This work contains not only hunting stories but also detailed instructions on how Pope made his bows, bowstrings, arrows, and broadheads. The book is still in print and is a very enjoyable read for those interested in the early years of the longbow in the United States.

Pope and Young weren't the only Americans to have adventurous lives with the longbow. Brothers Will and Maurice Thompson grew up with a love of the longbow and hunting in their hearts, and spent carefree lives pursuing their interests until both were called to serve the Confederacy during the Civil War (1861–1865). After the war was over, the brothers, as ex-Confederate soldiers, were forbidden from owning firearms. They soon found their way back to the bow and arrow, which provided them with the freedom for which they longed. The escapades of the Thompson brothers took place mainly in the swamps of Florida, where they hunted and lived off the land around them. The two also penned a book that is as well known as the one by Saxton Pope, *The Witchery of Archery*, published in 1923. Pope and Will Thompson also corresponded occasionally, swapping tales of the bow.

A MEDIEVAL WEAPON IN TODAY'S WORLD

Longbowmen still exist, just as in the days of Merry Olde England, although today we must contend with concrete jungles and crowded sidewalks. We seek out cool forests, sunlit glades, towering pines, lofty mountains, and the musical babblings of flowing brooks. For longbowmen, the bow itself is a means to an end, a tool without which we feel lost and out of touch with our own spirits.

Today, of course, there's no physical *need* for the longbow to procure food or to defend ourselves from hostile neighbors. If we want a nice juicy piece of meat, we just make a trip to the supermarket or butcher shop and pick out what we want. Firearms long ago replaced longbows as home or self-defense weapons. However, those of us who still shoot and hunt with the longbow today might argue that there is a deep-seated *psychological* need that can only be satisfied by time spent in the fields and woods, bow in hand. Perhaps this is a genetic trait passed on by our ancestors, who hunted their own meat and gathered their own herbs and vegetables. It's impossible to completely eliminate thousands of years of imprinted hunting and foraging habits. Or perhaps it's a personal or social trait that drives some of us to not only be alone in the wilds, but also to seek out others who think and feel along the same lines. It could be that the longbow represents a simple tool of a much simpler time, one without all of the stress and worry brought about by today's society. When we string up our longbows, shoulder quivers full of feathered shafts, and head for the woods, we achieve a freedom from all the distractions of the world in which we live. For many of us, the longbow has become a portal to another time where we can feel closer to life's natural processes and revive our spirits.

- 2 -

The Modern Longbow

Interest in traditional archery has grown by leaps and bounds over the last couple of decades, with new styles and models of longbows appearing regularly and bowyers popping up almost overnight. The sheer number of longbows available to today's archer is almost staggering, and things have certainly come a long way from when man first tied two ends of a stick together and discovered he could use it to make another stick fly.

EVOLUTION OF THE LONGBOW

The modern longbow evolved over the centuries from its Welsh, English, and Native American ancestors to become a much more efficient tool. Though the original designs are still widely used by many of today's archers, modern-day technologies such as epoxy glues and fiberglass enable longbows to better withstand rough treatment and the elements without loss of draw weight or the danger of exploding when shooting on a hot day. Design and materials have improved so much that it's no longer necessary to build a bow 6 feet long or more or to have a draw weight of 90 or 100 pounds in order to shoot farther, faster, and harder.

Saxton Pope and Arthur Young used bows made of yew, leaving the sapwood on to provide elasticity and help protect the bow from breaking. However, had the fiberglass and adhesive technologies we enjoy today been available to Pope and Young, I have a feeling they would gladly have used them. While faithful reproductions of many styles of Native American *flatbows* (shorter longbows with wide, thin limbs like recurve bows) and English-style longbows are still used by archers and bowhunters all over the world, the modern laminated longbow is a slightly different animal than its Welsh and English counterparts.

Through the early 1900s, the longbow was carved from a single stave of wood and subsequently known as a *selfbow*. Selfbows were—and still are—frequently backed by materials such as sinew or rawhide. A man named Howard Hill shared the same love of the longbow as Pope and Young. A highly educated man with the proper tools at his disposal, he experimented with different types of wood and laminated thin strips of wood together to add strength and cast to the longbow.

He initially made his yew longbows the same way Pope and Young did, but later began backing his bows with a species of bamboo. Hill noted that this backing made the bow faster and more efficient. He later heard of a man named Frank Eicholtz who was using a material called fiberglass to back his bows—this made the bow nearly indestructible. Hill sent two of his bows to Eicholtz to have fiberglass applied to the backs and fronts. The results were so impressive that Hill asked

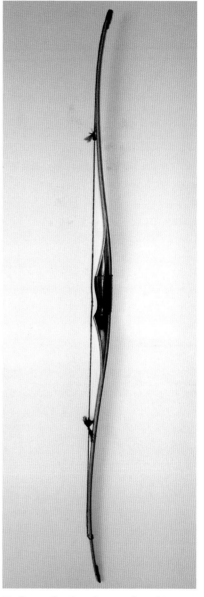

Deflex-reflex is a feature found in many modern longbows. It helps to make the bow more efficient and lessens hand shock.

Eicholtz to show him the process, and later used fiberglass on all the bows he made.

Hill did more to promote the longbow as a viable hunting tool than anyone else, and time and again proved it capable of almost unbelievable accuracy. He authored two books on hunting with the longbow, *Hunting the Hard Way* and *Wild Adventure*, both of which are still in print, as well as a full-length video of his African safari, called *Tembo*.

He referred to his style of longbow as the "American Straight End" longbow, as there was no deflex or reflex in the limbs. With *deflex-reflex*, the bow's limbs sweep gently back toward the archer, then back again toward the front of the bow. Later on, bowyers began building longbows with varying degrees of reflex and deflex, or both. Some bows today may have only one or the other; others depart radically enough from the profile of the longbow that they're known as hybrids.

LONGBOWS VERSUS RECURVES

On a longbow, the bowstring only touches the bow at each tip. If the bowstring touches part of the limb before it gets to the end of the limb tip, the bow is classified as a *recurve*. Recurve bows are easily distinguished from longbows by the graceful, pronounced sweep of their limb tips. Perhaps the easiest way to tell if you're looking at a longbow or recurve bow is to see if the bowstring touches the limbs anywhere besides the string nocks at the limb tips. On every recurve, the bowstring will touch a portion of both the upper and lower limbs, where the curves occur. The physical contact between the bowstring and limbs causes this particular style of bow to produce more noise at the shot. Also, as a recurve bow is drawn the limbs seem to unfold, while on the longbow they simply bend in a graceful arc.

Many people ask why I prefer the longbow, since the recurve is almost sure to shoot harder and faster because of the added energy stored in the recurved limbs. However, there are many advantages to the longbow, at least for me. The longbow is lighter in physical weight for the most part, which makes a big difference when you're covering a lot of ground on a hunt. Longbows also are a lot more forgiving of a *bad release*, when you fail to release the bowstring cleanly, which occurs more frequently during a high-pressure shot at a game animal than while on the target range where you are more relaxed and can take your time with a shot.

The limbs of the longbow are also narrower and thicker than those of a recurve, which means a longbow limb is less delicate. It's nearly impossible for a limb to develop a twist, which could cause those particular layers to delaminate. *Delamination* occurs when the adhesive holding the different veneers or fiberglass strips together fails and the veneers and lamination come apart.

The longbow also seems to be more efficient than a recurve, as it is better able to transfer the energy stored in its limbs at full draw and can shoot a heavier arrow harder than a recurve bow can. In the case of a hunting bow, speed is only one of the factors in the equation of efficiency. On the target range, a bow's ability to shoot an arrow in a flat trajectory is more important than its ability to transfer energy, which equates to penetration when hunting game animals.

CONSTRUCTION

In Pope and Young's time, and early on in Howard Hill's career, there was no shelf on the side of the bow to sit the arrow on while drawing and shooting. The arrow simply rested on the knuckle of the bow hand, with a small piece of leather on the handle to protect the bow from the arrow's passing.

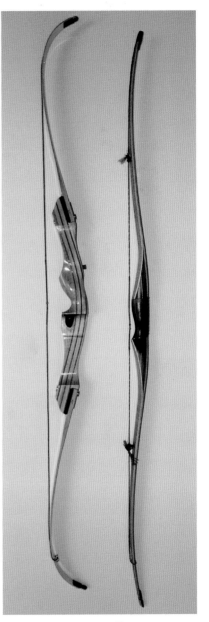

One of the obvious differences between longbows and recurves is the sweep of the upper limp tips in the recurve.

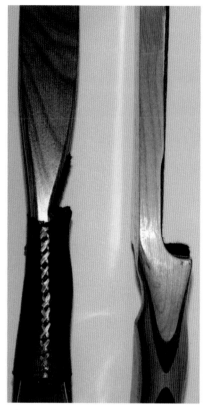

The depth of the arrow shelf can vary. The closer the shelf is cut to the center of the bow, the less arrow spine is required.

Later, a small piece of wood or leather was glued to the side of the bow to serve as an *arrow rest*, or *arrow shelf*. Today, nearly every traditional bow made has a rest built into the bow itself. Black Widow custom bows feature a "relieved" arrow shelf, with the edge of the shelf cut back a bit to prevent the *fletching*—the feathers glued to the arrow shaft for guidance—from striking the area as the arrow passes.

The distance the shelf is cut from the center of the bow, or the *shelf depth*, determines how close the arrow lies to the center of the bow and how stiff the *arrow spine* needs to be. Arrow spine is determined by both the diameter and the length of the arrow. The shorter the arrow, the stiffer its spine.

While most longbows today are built with the shelf cut ⅛ inch past center, there are bows made with deeper shelf cuts. A longbow with a shelf cut only ⅛ inch past center will require an arrow with less spine, or stiffness, than a longbow with a deeper shelf because the arrow will need to flex more as it bends around the *riser*—the vertical section of the bow above the arrow shelf—and leaves the bowstring. (If you shoot in International Bowhunting Organization (IBO) tournaments, remember that in order for a longbow to qualify under IBO rules, the shelf cannot be cut past center and you must use wooden arrows; otherwise you will be required to shoot in a different bow class.)

Many years ago, bows were glued using forms and "hot boxes" to cure the epoxy. This process remains largely unchanged today. Laminated bows are made of thin strips of fiberglass and wood veneers that are then coated with epoxy glue and placed in a form that will create the profile shape of the bow when the glue dries. Clamps applied to the form hold the laminates in place. The form is then placed in an oven to allow the epoxy glue to dry and cure.

Depending on the manufacturer, however, the process of shaping the bow's handle and cutting out the limb tapers is sometimes done by a computer-aided drafting machine as an automated process. Essentially the only component of modern traditional bow building that cannot be done by machine is *tillering* the limbs, or shaping them so that they exert an equal amount of force.

Bowstrings also have come a long way since the days when they were made of linen thread or plant fibers like hemp or flax. Later, bowstrings were made of

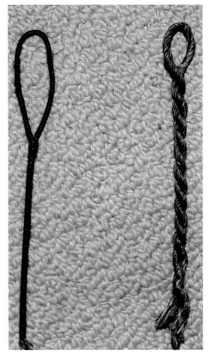

Strings for the longbow can be either endless loop (left) or Flemish style (right). I prefer the Flemish style for its durability.

Dacron, a stronger and longer-lasting material that has quite a bit of stretch. Reinforced tips on most modern longbows allow for the use of the same synthetic string materials as those used on compound bows, providing a bit more arrow speed, a lot less stretch, and a longer-lasting bowstring. Fast Flight, Astro Flight, and DynaFlight 97 are common trade names for synthetic string material. However, using these bowstrings on longbows not made with reinforced limb tips will cause damage to your bow and could possibly injure you. If you have an older longbow or don't know if your bow will accept synthetic bowstrings, stick with Dacron.

Dacron strings can be made in two styles—*endless loop* or *Flemish*. The endless loop style is made by forming a large loop with a continuous length of string material.

A LONGBOW TOO LONG

Several years ago, when I first started shooting and hunting exclusively with the longbow, I was under the mistaken impression that longer was better. Everything I'd read on the subject up to that point conveyed the idea that a longbow had to be long—at least 68 inches, which seemed to be the ideal length for that particular style of bow. I had no idea that there were other models out there that would better suit my needs, and besides, I wanted to do it the old-fashioned way.

Prior to deer season, I had located a grove of white oaks and placed a stand there to take advantage of the whitetail's tendency to gobble up the sweet mast that littered the ground beneath those stately old trees. One fine evening, as the magical hour drew near, I noticed several deer working in my direction through the woods. While it was a bit early in the season for bucks to be moving, I wasn't worried. The state of Indiana allows two deer to be taken with the bow, and I had every intention of bringing home a nice big doe for the freezer and then spending the rest of the season looking for a buck.

As luck would have it, all eight deer were does, and the largest of the bunch paused near the base of my tree to munch acorns as the rest filed past to another tree. This was my first hunt with the new 68-inch longbow and I badly wanted to make meat and be able to consider myself a true longbow hunter. The doe was no more than 10 feet from

Wear-resistant serving material is then used to create the string loops at each end, which go over the string nock. The Flemish style is made up of two or three bundles of string material that are braided and twisted so that the end loops don't separate. It's easy to recognize because of the thicker section of string at each end caused by the braiding process.

With both styles, string length is changed by either twisting or untwisting the bowstring to shorten or lengthen it. When using

A LONGBOW TOO LONG

the tree I was in, amounting to what I considered a slam-dunk shot. But as I raised my bow to draw, I made a horrible discovery: No matter how I twisted and contorted, there was no way I could get a shot at the deer because the bottom limb on my longbow would strike the tree stand platform! To try it would mean taking an irresponsible shot and risking either wounding the doe and not recovering her, or breaking the bottom limb on my new bow. "That's okay," I thought to myself. "I'll wait until she works her way to the right side, and my bottom limb will be clear of the stand because I tilt the bow to the right when I shoot." It was a good plan . . . right up until I realized that even though my bottom limb was in the clear, my top limb would hit the tree.

Later, I furthered my education on the longbow and did hours of research on what was available from different bowyers across the country. After selecting a bowyer whose product looked like it would fit my needs, I chose a 62-inch model and eagerly awaited its arrival. I realize that 6 inches doesn't sound like much, especially when it amounts to 3 inches at each end of the bow, but that change made all the difference in the world. I've never again had a problem with limb clearance in any situation. As a matter of fact, I've scaled back even more and now own several longbows in both the 62-inch and 60-inch classes. These bows give up nothing in the way of performance and suit my hunting style perfectly.

Flemish-style string on your longbow, make sure you don't untwist it too many times or the string will separate, as the twist is what holds it together. No matter what material your bowstring is made of, be sure to keep it well waxed with a quality string wax to lengthen its life and help protect it from abrasion. It's also a good practice to always carry a spare bowstring that has been "shot-in" and is identical to the one on your bow.

- 3 -

Finding a Longbow That's Right for You

In order to determine what style of longbow best suits your needs, it's important to know what you're going to ask it to do. Some people love to shoot longbows simply for the pleasure of watching their arrows fly. Others enjoy wandering the woods and fields, looking for targets such as rotting stumps and leaves to shoot at with arrows tipped with Judo points or blunts. Still others are serious 3D target shooters. Some are bowhunters. The majority of people who shoot a longbow participate in all the above. Personally, I own several longbows and shoot every day, although I only use three of them regularly. All three are capable of everything I call on them to do, are reflex-deflex in profile with draw weights between 65 and 68 pounds, are between 60 and 62 inches in length, and are equipped with synthetic strings.

CHOOSING A LONGBOW

You might say that choosing a longbow is a lot like choosing a spouse. There's the initial awkwardness when you're trying to be on your best behavior. Then, as you become more comfortable around each other, you begin to complement one another. No, I'm not talking about actual *compliments* like "That dress really brings out the blue in your eyes." I'm talking about the point when your skills and the bow's potential begin to come together, and you start to understand what your longbow needs from you in order to do its job. I will stick by this statement: Each and every bow has its own personality and quirks, just like a person, regardless of whether it was made by a custom bowyer or rolled off the assembly line in an archery plant. It's up to you to learn from your new hunting partner and adapt to its qualities and limitations, just like in any other relationship. In doing so, you will realize your full potential as a longbow shooter.

Before choosing your longbow, you should know your draw weight and draw length. *Draw weight* is the amount of weight, measured in pounds, that it takes to draw the bowstring back to the industry standard of 28 inches. For every inch above or below 28 inches, you gain or lose 2 to 3 pounds of draw weight, respectively. *Draw length* is measured as the distance in inches from the bottom of the arrow nock groove to the point where the arrow passes over the far side of the shelf when you are at full draw. Knowing your draw length and how much draw weight you're actually pulling is essential information for choosing the correct arrow and obtaining the best

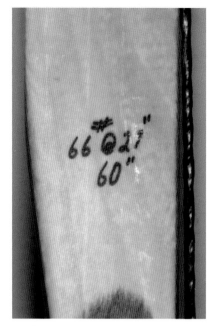

The draw weight of the bow and the draw length at which the weight was measured are marked on all manufactured longbows. For every inch above or below the draw length shown on the bow, add or subtract 2 to 3 pounds of draw weight, respectively.

arrow flight possible. It's also very important to remember that if you're switching from a compound bow to a longbow, your draw length will be a couple of inches shorter. Longbows have no "let off" at full draw—your shoulders don't expand or stretch out at full draw as they do with a compound, but instead remain compressed.

There are a few general rules that apply to the longbow, regardless of whether you use it for hunting, 3D target shoots, stump shooting, or target and field archery.

1. **The longer the overall length of your longbow, the smoother the draw will be.** The draw length can reach up to 28 or 29 inches. The longer limb length allows for a smoother distribution of the draw weight throughout as you draw.

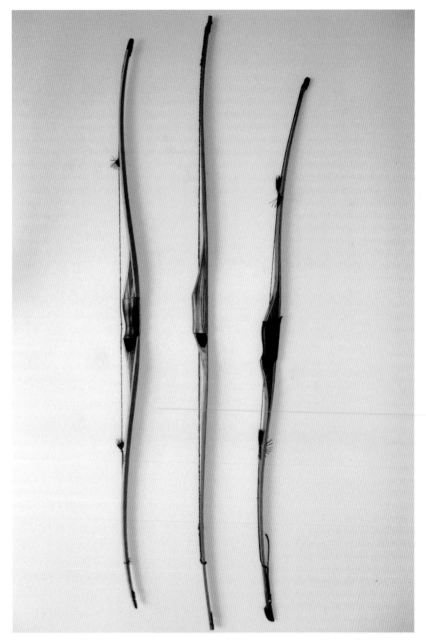

The modern longbow is available in lengths from 58 to 72 inches, offering options for shooters of all draw sizes.

2. **For 3D or target archery, a longbow with a draw weight of 35 to 45 pounds will be plenty in most cases.** The target arrows you shoot will be lighter than hunting arrows, making a heavy draw weight unnecessary. Lighter arrows fly farther and flatter, allowing you a greater margin for error in case you misjudge the distance to the target. The lighter draw weight also enables you to shoot for hours without tiring.

3. **For hunting, choose an overall bow length based on your physical height.** Longbows are available in lengths from about 58 inches all the way up to 72 inches. I'm 5 feet 7 inches tall and my draw length is 27 inches. Keep in mind that longer bows are more difficult to shoot from a tree stand because the platform may interfere with the lower limb of your bow when making shots close to your stand. My three favorite bows are between 60 and 62 inches in length, and I've never had a problem shooting with them from tree stands or ground blinds.

4. **Hunting arrows should have at least 8 grains of arrow weight per pound of bow weight.** In other words, if you're drawing a bow that's 50 pounds at your draw length, your arrow should weigh at least 400 grains. The heavier the better, up to the point where the weight becomes a detriment to arrow flight.

3D and Target-Shooting Bows

If you plan to use your longbow specifically for 3D shoots or any type of target archery, whether in the field or backyard, the most important consideration is having a bow that you can shoot accurately and repeatedly in various weather conditions. This means that draw weight is much less of a factor and that light arrows are an advantage. This also means that bow length won't cause many problems, although most 3D events usually have a few shots that require you to bend, kneel, or otherwise contort your body to get a clear shot at the target.

The point of most target shoots is to re-create hunting conditions when the distance to the target is unknown to you beforehand and varies between targets. Target shooting is the most realistic method of practicing for bow season, and bowhunters take advantage of 3D shoots to help hone their skills. However, there are plenty of traditional 3D shooters who will never draw their bows on big game animals and simply love just shooting their bows. The combination of the proper

MEASURING YOUR DRAW LENGTH

There are a couple of ways to measure your draw length. The first—and easiest—is to visit an archery pro shop and tell the employee that you would like to have your draw length measured. Make sure you inform him or her that you'll be shooting a longbow with your fingers. The staff member should be familiar with the shooting stance and form for a traditional bow and can determine your draw length with the aid of a *draw check bow*, a very light draw weight bow that has a permanently attached arrow marked with a scale in inches.

The other method requires only a wall and a tape measure. Make a closed fist with the hand that will be holding the bow and press the front of your fist against a wall. Take up a stance as though you're drawing a bow, bringing your drawing hand back to place the middle finger in the corner of your mouth, the most common anchor point location used by longbow shooters. Using the tape measure, record the distance from the wall at the front of your fist to the point at the corner of your mouth where your middle finger is anchored.

I keep a small notebook in my archery tackle box with important measurements like my draw length, arrow length, and other information specific to each bow I own.

longbow and arrows will help you shoot as efficiently as possible and allow you to achieve consistent accuracy, which is the name of the game no matter what your favorite longbow activity.

Hunting Bows

If you plan to use your longbow for hunting, you need to pick one that has enough draw weight to ensure complete penetration in whatever game you're hunting. The most common big game animals pursued by hunters here in the United States are deer (whitetails, mule deer, and blacktails), elk, moose, wild boar, black bear, mountain lions, and occasionally sheep and goats in the mountains. A good longbow for the bowhunter should be as short as you can shoot comfortably, easy to maneuver with through thick brush, and sturdy enough to withstand weather of all kinds and the occasional ding and accidental abuse that are natural parts of the rigors of the hunt. No matter how careful you try to be, there will be the inevitable accident when your bow falls over and lands in a pile of rubble, you smack it against a rock outcropping, or you drop it from a tree stand . . . the list goes on and on. As time passes, you'll recall each of these dings and scratches and how they got there, much like a battle-hardened old warrior recalls how he got each of the scars he bears with pride.

There are a great many opinions on how much draw weight is needed to bring down big game. It has often been said that a bow pulling 55 pounds will bring down any big game animal in North America. I will add a caveat to that: A 55-pound bow *may* bring down any big game animal in North America, *provided* a quality, razor-sharp broadhead is used and mounted on a heavy arrow that flies straight. The shot also must enter a vital area (the chest cavity should always be the main target), preferably with a complete pass-through. I don't necessarily mean that the arrow goes completely through the animal and exits out the other side to bury itself in the ground—although that's generally the case for a good shot through the chest cavity—but rather that the broadhead itself pierces both sides of the chest cavity. (I'll talk more about bowhunting in chapter 12.)

MODERN VARIATIONS

As I covered briefly in the previous chapter, there are four main variations of the longbow available today: the selfbow, the straight longbow, the deflex-reflex style, and the flatbow.

Selfbow

The simple selfbow, the type used by the Thompson brothers and Pope and Young, is made of a single stave of wood with no fiberglass laminations. Depending on your choice of bowyer (and there are many who make beautiful bows), you can have your selfbow backed with snakeskin, rawhide, sinew, or nothing at all, depending on the type of wood used. Having the bow backed adds strength to the wood and helps prevent it from developing splinters. Depending on the type and amount of backing, it can contribute a little power to the bow, but its primary function is integrity.

Since selfbows have no glass laminations, they are not compatible with low-stretch synthetic strings such as Fast Flight. More importantly, since selfbows are each handmade one at a time, they have a tendency to be expensive, which can be prohibitive if you're on a limited budget.

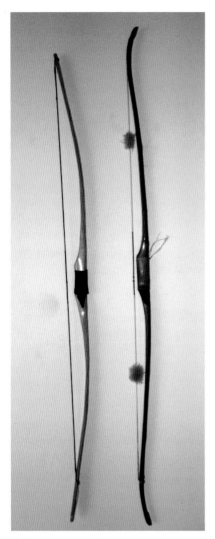

Selfbows are made from a single piece of wood called a bowstave. They can be unbacked, like the Osage orange bow (left), or backed with natural materials such as sinew and hide glue, like the hickory selfbow (right). Deflex can also be added to the limb tips using heat, as shown in the Osage orange bow.

After gaining some experience with a selfbow, you may decide to start building your own, an extremely rewarding experience. There are plenty of books and even a few classes available on the subject if that's where your interests lie.

Straight Longbow

The next variation is the straight longbow, which has no deflex or reflex in the limbs. This style of longbow is very popular with fans of Howard Hill, who went into business building this type of bow and made a living shooting it as well as successfully killing many big game animals including elephants, Cape buffalo, lions, and tigers. Of course, we may never see another archer with Hill's natural talent, but if this bow style was good enough for him, it's good enough, period.

The straight, or straight-end, longbow is capable of shooting a heavy arrow with a lot of punch, which is extremely important if you're a bowhunter. Too many times archers (even traditional archers) get caught up in the arrow speed craze. It has been proven many times over the years that arrow speed is only part of the equation when it comes to wringing out every bit of a longbow's efficiency. A heavy arrow absorbs more of the bow's energy than a light arrow does. When shooting a light arrow from a longbow with a heavier draw weight, part of the energy from the bow remains in the bow after the shot because the arrow simply doesn't have enough mass to absorb all the energy. This leftover energy is felt as hand shock and, depending on the amount, can be very unpleasant. Another way to look at it is to compare throwing a rubber ball and then a very heavy rock. The rubber ball takes very little energy to throw and travels fairly fast for a longer distance, while the heavy rock takes more effort, drains your arm of more energy, and doesn't travel nearly as far as the rubber ball. Even though the rubber ball can be thrown farther at a much faster velocity and the heavy rock doesn't travel very fast or very far, the rock carries more energy than the ball simply because the rock has more mass and is capable of absorbing more of the kinetic energy imparted by your arm during the throw. Think of it like this: Which hits harder, a feather going 300 feet per second or a telephone pole traveling 175 feet per second?

Deflex-Reflex Longbow

The third variation in longbow limb design is the deflex-reflex style. Remember, this means that

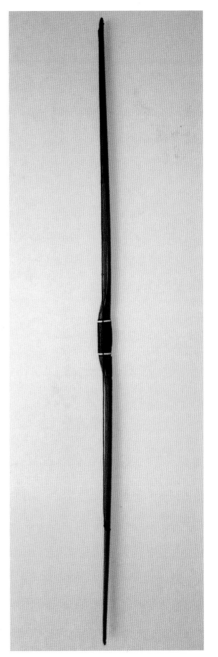

A version of Howard Hill's straight-end American longbow.

the limbs leave the handle and curve gently back toward the shooter, then curve back the other way toward the limb tips. The advantage to this style, as I've discovered over the years, is that it is more efficient, providing more energy to the arrow as well as reducing the hand shock felt. Hand shock is generally the product of one or two problems: either faulty bow design or an arrow that is too light to absorb the bow's energy. While hand shock may not bother some shooters, it can have a detrimental effect on joints, ligaments, and tendons.

I've also found that deflex-reflex bows are smoother to draw in shorter lengths than a straight longbow because the draw weight is distributed more throughout the limb, enabling some shooters to use a shorter overall bow length. In a straight longbow, only about half of the limb flexes when the bow is drawn.

Flatbow

The last style is the flatbow, which has a handle and riser section similar to that of a longbow. However, the limbs on a flatbow are wide and thin, much like the limbs on a recurve bow, as opposed to the thick, narrow limbs found on most longbows. Many of the bows used by Native Americans were classified as flatbows because they were short and had wide limbs, which enabled Native American hunters to shoot accurately from horseback and avoid hitting their horse's side or their own leg when at full draw. Modern flatbows are constructed of laminations just like a longbow and may have deflex or reflex in the limbs. Flatbows are generally shorter in overall length than longbows, averaging about 62 inches.

Flatbows are simply another longbow design, and while certain models may be a little more efficient (as can be the case with any bow style), the decision to shoot a flatbow is merely one of personal preference.

GRIPS

Handle size and shape are features that can make a difference between whether a bow is comfortable to shoot or uncomfortable in your hand. Except for minor variances in hand shape, mass-produced bows of the same model all have roughly the same size and shape grips.

If you decide on a custom-made longbow, you may have a choice between grip sizes and shapes. There are two basic variations of the grip on a longbow: the pistol grip and the straight grip. Longbows with pistol grips will typically have bigger riser sections around the arrow

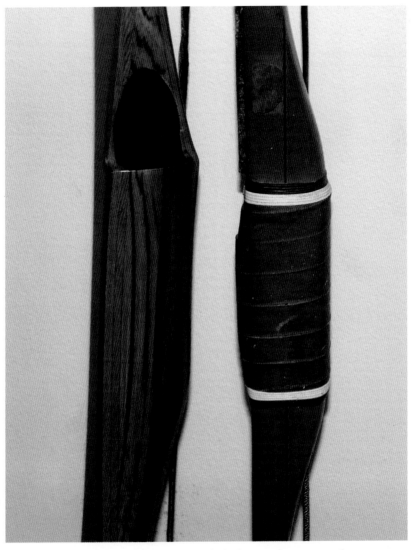

The "broom handle" grip (right) has no dish shape or locator notch.

shelf and the same style of grip as seen on many recurve bows. The straight grip, commonly called the "broom handle" grip, has very little of the contour seen on a pistol grip. The straight grip may have a slight depression, known as a *locator grip*, below the arrow shelf. The locator grip allows you to grip the bow in the same spot each time and helps ensure consistency between shots.

Locator grips (left) help ensure that you're gripping the same location each time. Some bowyers offer custom-shaped grips on their longbows (right).

Some longbow grips are covered with leather and others are covered with a rubber sleeve, while some have nothing at all over the grip.

The circumference of the grip is also a determining factor in how comfortable the bow is to shoot. If you have small hands, a longbow with a "fat" grip might make you feel as though you're going to drop the bow when releasing the arrow. Instinctive shooting requires concentration, and it's hard to concentrate when you're afraid of dropping your bow.

The only custom bowyer I've ever spoken to who took an interest in the size and shape of my hand was Ron King, owner and bowyer of Fox Archery in Wallowa, Oregon. When I placed my order, Ron asked me to trace my hand on a piece of paper and send it along with the order. When my Fox longbow arrived, it felt very much as though the bow had been made specifically to fit my hand—which, in fact, it was. Another longbow that fits my hand extremely well is my TimberHawk longbow, made by firefighter Scott Mitchell from Bloomington, Indiana, not far up the road from my house. My TimberHawk bow features a palm swell on the left side of the bow (I'm right-handed), and though not extreme in size, it fills my hand enough to provide a very comfortable feeling of control without causing torque, one of the major causes of "misdirected arrows" and a prime accuracy-robbing culprit.

TAKEDOWN LONGBOW

Another very important option to consider, especially if you're a traveling bowhunter, is a takedown bow. Available in two- or three-piece options, takedown bows allow you to disassemble the bow for easy packing when traveling by vehicle or airplane to a far-off destination. Some archers have the misconception that takedown bows are somehow structurally weaker or not as efficient as a one-piece longbow. This was perhaps the case when takedown longbows were first being manufactured, but no longer. Takedown bows are just as sturdy as a one-piece longbow, with no loss of performance. Being able to disassemble your longbow and store it in your baggage is a definite advantage if you're flying to Alaska or Africa, not only because it will be cheaper but also because you can store the bow in a hard case packed in your luggage and won't need to worry about it surviving the trip.

The new rage in traditional bows is a type of takedown bow that has synthetic risers and is drilled for a cushion plunger, rest, sights, and almost any other aftermarket gadget an archer could want, giving it infinitely more tuning options. The arrow shelves on these bows are cut well past center and, just like compound bows, can be set up with an arrow rest or a cushion plunger to fine-tune arrow flight. Or you can shoot them *off the shelf*, without any type of arrow rest, simply covering the arrow shelf and sight window instead with a material such as thin leather or one of the self-adhesive shelf rest materials widely available. The limbs for this style of takedown bow are also adjustable for tiller and available in different lengths to suit any shooter.

- 4 -

Custom versus Mass-Produced Longbows

The longbow is wonderful in that you can invest as little or as much as you want in your purchase, depending on the intended purpose, and still have a bow that suits both your needs and wants. When I put away the recurve and started shooting only the longbow many years ago, I started out with an entry-level model that was as close as I could come to what I'd seen in books and magazines.

From what I knew of longbows at the time (which wasn't all that much), they were "supposed" to be 68 inches in length and have a narrow handle and narrow, thick limbs. With my limited resources, I finally settled on a model that I thought would be perfect for me, so I ordered an "off-the-shelf" name-brand longbow through the local sporting goods dealer. When it arrived, I thought the bow was perfect—a piece of art. It was 68 inches long and drew 65 pounds at 28 inches, according to the writing on the bow. I took it home and immediately began shooting.

As with most things, once you look at them with a critical eye, you'll notice imperfections. This was no different. At some point, I slid my hand down the outside of the top limb and felt a sharp stick. Upon closer inspection, I saw a splinter in the grain of the wood sandwiched between the clear fiberglass laminations. Instead of being paper smooth, the wood was apparently sanded very little at the factory in an attempt to keep the draw weight of the bow higher. After carefully removing the splinter, I continued shooting but couldn't stop thinking that maybe I should look at the bow a little more closely. I also discovered that in the time between bringing the bow home and shooting it for a week or so that the fiberglass lamination on the back of the bow had split at the point where the shelf rest had been cut.

I immediately took the bow back to the dealer where I bought it. He called the manufacturer, who told him it was "nothing to worry about and would not affect the performance of the longbow." Luckily, the dealer was reputable and chose to make it right, ordering another bow for me. When this one arrived, I checked the finish work on the limb edges before even taking it home. This bow was only slightly better than the last one, but I wanted to get back to shooting, so I took it home. Not a week later, the fiberglass on the back of the bow split in exactly the same spot as the first one. That was a hard lesson for me because I'd never had a problem with my recurve bows, other than a twisted limb that occurred because I was stringing and unstringing it improperly (another hard lesson). The bow would have been fine for someone less serious about archery or someone who didn't shoot as much as me, but it was clear that if I was going to be satisfied, I'd have to put up the money for the quality I wanted and needed. I saved up and invested in a Black Widow longbow that was custom made for me with a draw weight that ended up being 63 pounds at my personal draw length of 27 inches. Since then I've acquired several custom longbows and along the way have discovered exactly what I want and need in a bow.

OFF-THE-SHELF LONGBOWS

When choosing a longbow, you must decide if you want a mass-produced, "off-the-shelf" model or a custom, handmade longbow. When I use the term "off-the-shelf," it's not meant to be discriminatory or defaming in any way. It just means that the bows are turned out in great numbers in a large factory and thus can be mass-produced cheaply, keeping the cost of the bow down for the consumer. This has obvious advantages if you're on a budget, and the quality and workmanship of mass-produced bows have come a long way since when I first started shooting them. Martin Archery and Bear Archery are two names that are probably familiar as being top producers of quality longbows.

I recently interviewed Neil Byce, whose father was one of Fred Bear's original bowyers at the Bear Archery plant in Grayling, Michigan, and who later made the move with the company to Gainesville, Florida, where the plant remains in full production today. While discussing the mass production of traditional bows, Byce was quick to point out that although some machines (the same ones, in fact, designed and built by Fred Bear at the original plant in Grayling) are used in the

The longbow on the far left is an "off-the-shelf" bow, while the two on the right are custom made. Many large companies that mass-produce traditional longbows have increased the quality of their product in response to the resurgence in the use of traditional bows.

creation of their traditional bows, there hasn't been a machine built yet that can tiller those limbs and get them to draw to center. This part of the process is still done by hand by skilled craftsmen and women. Mr. Byce also said that each handle on every traditional wood bow is still shaped by hand, and that no two are exactly the same. In essence, even though Bear traditional bows are built in assembly-line fashion, each is still inspected by hand and bears unique qualities that make it different from any other bow of the same make and model. In other words, every Bear traditional bow is "custom" in its own way.

A ready-made bow can be ordered easily and you can be shooting it in just a few days, whereas a custom-made longbow usually takes several weeks to complete because it's handmade to order, from glue-up to final finishing. If you have the opportunity to handle and shoot the model prior to ordering it, you know what to expect when it arrives. On the other hand, if you simply picked the longbow out of a lineup, thinking it looked good and met all the requirements you were looking for, you may be in for an unpleasant surprise when it arrives in the mail. For instance, the grip may not be as comfortable as you were expecting, or it may be higher or lower than you expected, forcing you to make small changes in your shooting style. In most instances, these differences can be overcome with a little tape here and there to bring the grip shape around to where it's comfortable. Also, sometimes the bow you ordered may not look the same as the one shown in the catalog, even though it's the same make and model, because of differences in wood coloration and the like.

CUSTOM LONGBOWS

If a custom longbow is more to your liking, be prepared to spend anywhere from $500 to well over $1,000, depending on the bowyer. Traditional archery has experienced a phenomenal resurgence in popularity during the last decade, and the number of bowyers has increased in kind. Ask a dozen different longbow shooters who makes the best longbow, and you'll get a dozen different answers. It seems that every bow company has a legion of loyal fans. I can only speak of the ones I've had experience with: Black Widow Bows in Nixa, Missouri; Fox Archery in Wallowa, Oregon; Martin Archery in Walla Walla, Washington; and TimberHawk Bows in Bloomington, Indiana. For what it's worth, the three bows in my current arsenal that see the lion's share of work are the two by Fox Archery and the one by TimberHawk. As I stated earlier, I've had several custom bows over the years and never found the need to go elsewhere.

When choosing a custom longbow, it's paramount that you know what you plan to do with the bow and what you will expect of it. Certain woods appear beautiful on the bow but may not offer the best options for speed, durability, and repeated use. Talk to as many custom bowyers as you can and shoot their bows if at all possible. All bowyers worth their salt will have a list of customers willing to talk about the longbow they purchased from that company. Their best advertising is word of mouth. Talk to a good cross section of customers, both those who were pleased with their longbows and those who were dissatisfied. Find out why they didn't like their custom longbows and what problems they experienced, and try to determine if the issue was with the bow or the shooter. Too many shooters new to traditional archery make the mistake of buying a longbow with too much draw weight. They think that since they can shoot a 70-pound compound all day long, they should be able to shoot a 70-pound longbow just as easily. Remember, there is no let off with a traditional longbow, and you use a different set of muscles when drawing and anchoring.

One of the benefits of purchasing a custom bow is the fact that bowyers are interested in pleasing you, the customer, and will bend over backward to make sure you are pleased with your bow. Good ones will ask lots of questions about how you shoot, what you'll be doing with the bow, and what you expect from the bow. They should ask about what kind of grip you want, and many will even offer to reproduce the grip on your favorite bow if you'll send it to them.

This isn't to say that custom bows don't have their problems. I once owned a high-dollar custom takedown recurve in which the pins that centered the limbs on the handle all fell out when I took off the limbs. Then there was the custom longbow that broke right in the middle as I came to full draw on a whitetail doe. I once ordered a longbow from a custom bow maker that, when it arrived, had a twist in the upper limb, and the limb tips looked as though they had been finished with a coarse rasp. The bow had horrible hand shock, and I eventually traded it for a dozen arrows.

The bottom line is that there are benefits and drawbacks to *both* sides of the custom versus mass-produced question. For that reason, it

USED BOWS—A WORD OF CAUTION

I used to do quite a lot of 3D tournament archery shooting as an associate shooter for Martin Archery through a local dealer. My circuit wasn't huge, but at that time the whole 3D archery business was growing by leaps and bounds. Naturally, as a traditional shooter and longbowman, I gravitated toward other shooters who also used traditional bows.

Back then, custom bows were well out of my reach, but I wanted one so badly I could taste it. At one of the shoots I attended regularly, the individual who owned the land and sponsored the shoot also had a small pro shop where shooters could pick up various odds and ends they may have forgotten at home. Or, if something broke on the range while shooting, a quick trip back to the pro shop would put them back in the game.

There were several bows displayed on the wall inside the pro shop: trade-ins, ready-to-shoot bows, and the like. But there was one bow that caught my eye because it was a stickbow—an Appalachian Mountain flatbow, to be exact. Wow! A real live custom stickbow, right here in this little Podunk shack in the middle of nowhere. I casually asked the proprietor how much he would take for the bow (in retrospect, I should have asked how much he was going to take me for), and he replied that since I was a regular at his shoots, he would let me have it for $75. Trying my best to contain my excitement—and not doing a very good job of it—I promised to return next weekend with the cash. Being a true salesman, the man behind the counter said he had two or three other people looking at the bow but that if I really wanted it, he'd take it down off display and put it in the "back room." I couldn't imagine where the back room might have been, as the shack consisted of only one room, but I agreed and returned the next week, money in hand and anticipation in my heart.

pays to do all the homework you can on whatever longbow you're interested in, and to speak to as many people as you can who actually own that type of bow.

One source for finding advertisements for traditional bow makers is *Traditional Bowhunter,* an entertaining and instructive magazine and

USED BOWS—A WORD OF CAUTION *continued*

Once money and merchandise had changed hands, I couldn't wait to get home to try out my new prize. The bow itself was gorgeous, if a bit weather-beaten, but I figured a few coats of Tru-Oil would restore the luster to this beauty. The bowstring seemed a bit fuzzy from wear, but it was real no-kiddin' Fast Flight and a liberal dose of string wax would take care of the fuzziness. As soon as I got home, I set the bow up and moved the nocking point on the string to about where I thought it should be. The first arrow was a disaster. It barely stuck in the target from 15 yards out. The second wasn't much better. The bow was marked 63 pounds at 28 inches, so I knew it should have enough power to launch my arrows a lot faster than they were going. As I continued to shoot, I began to notice a slight "ticking" noise each time I drew the bow. When I sat down to give the bow a good going-over—something I should've done before I ever laid down the cash—I noticed that a wide section of the grain had lifted from the face of the bow about two-thirds of the way up from the riser. Someone had obviously glued it back down, hoping the next fool who looked at the bow wouldn't notice. Well, I didn't notice and, being the next fool, had purchased a bow that was absolutely useless for either target shooting or hunting. Not wanting to pass my bad fortune on to someone else, I leaned the bow unceremoniously in a back corner of the garage. It remained there as a lesson until I decided it had no more to teach me and used it for kindling in the fire ring in my backyard. My daughters and I made s'mores, and I wondered if they realized the true cost of that fire.

The lesson here is to never buy a used bow until you've gone over it with a fine-toothed comb, found out who the previous owner was, and shot at least a couple dozen of your own arrows through it. There are much cheaper ways to build a fire to make s'mores!

the best place short of the internet to find a bowyer that might fill your needs. The most important thing to remember when buying a longbow is this: If you buy cheap, you get cheap. Do a lot of research, handle and shoot as many different longbows as possible before buying, and remember: *Caveat emptor!*

- 5 -

Arrows, Arrows, and More Arrows

Some longbow enthusiasts are so preoccupied with the bow itself that they lose track of the whole purpose of the longbow—that is, to launch an arrow. I admit to being a member of that fraternity early on because I thought that when I finally bought a custom longbow, all my problems would magically be eliminated by the sheer awesomeness of the bow itself. Wrong. The truth of the matter is you can have the best, most expensive longbow in the world, but without the correct arrow to shoot from it, you may as well have a tree limb with a piece of bailing twine tied to it. One the other end of the equation, you can take that same tree limb with bailing twine for a bowstring and, with a properly spined arrow, have a very efficient bow. The arrow is the key to success, but it has to be the *right* arrow!

It's critical to know your draw length—otherwise you may end up with an arrow that's too short or longer than necessary. It's always better to start out with a shaft that's too long so that you can shorten it if need be. You can't add length to an arrow that's already too short. My rule of thumb when buying arrows is to get a length that is 2 inches longer than my draw length. This is because I'm a bowhunter. Remember, my fingers are on the other side of that arrow shelf, and I don't want to lose one if I happen to overdraw my bow slightly in the heat of the moment while hunting.

Once you've determined your arrow length, you'll have to find the proper arrow spine, choose from the three basic arrow materials available—wood, aluminum, and carbon—and select your points.

SPINE

Luckily, it didn't take me long to figure out that you can't (in most cases) shoot the same arrows meant for different bows without some adjustments, even if the bows are the same draw weight. I had a basic understanding of arrow spine from my recurve days, but hadn't taken into account the fact that my recurves were all centershot, with the arrow shelf cut far enough past the centerline of the bow that it was very forgiving of arrow spine problems.

The longbow is a much different matter. If you put an arrow on the bowstring of a right-handed bow, hold the bow straight vertically, and sight down the arrow, you'll notice that the arrow points to the left of where the front of the bow is pointing instead of straight ahead. The fact that anybody can shoot an arrow straight with a longbow is a minor miracle when you consider that the arrow has to physically flex *around* the bow as it leaves the string. This little phenomenon, known as *Archer's paradox*, is what allows us to shoot straight and to do so accurately and repeatedly—*if* we use an arrow that is correctly spined, that is. This is why the stiffness of the arrow is one of the keys to good arrow flight. The arrow must flex as it passes the bow to clear the riser but still be stiff enough to straighten out quickly after it leaves the string. If the arrow shelf were cut past the centerline of the bow, the arrow would point the same direction as the front of the bow and stiffness would not be as big a factor. In other words, the closer to the center of the bow the arrow shelf is cut, the straighter the arrow will be in relation to the bow itself.

Arrow manufacturers supply spine charts that help you pick the correct arrow based on the draw weight of the bow and the weight of the field point or broadhead to be used, but arrow spine is so critical for traditional archery that choosing a shaft by using a spine chart is only going to get you in the ballpark. Individual bows and archers vary so much that the only thing that will work for you is . . . well, what works for you.

More weight on the front of the arrow will cause the arrow to flex more as the bowstring applies pressure from the rear. An arrow with too little spine will fly downrange with the back end of the arrow to the left and will strike the target with the back end to the left of the point of impact. An arrow that is too stiff, or that has too much spine, will fly downrange with the back end of the arrow to the right and will hit the target with the back end to the right of the point of impact. The key is to find a field point or broadhead weight that allows the arrow to fly straight downrange and impact straight in the target (see Chapter 10).

WOOD ARROWS

Arrows have been made from wood since the beginning of archery. River cane, witch hazel, bamboo, and various species of stiff grasses have all been used at one point or another throughout the centuries, but thankfully a process came along that allowed for the manufacture of wood shafts in more consistent sizes, weights, and spines. Wood arrows are obviously the most traditional of all arrow materials, but they are also the most work. Port-Orford-cedar is by far the favored wood, but arrows are also made from fir, lodgepole pine, and heavier, denser woods such as hickory. Even the $3/8$-inch wood dowels available at most hardware stores can be fashioned into heavy, high-quality arrows capable of taking big, tough game animals from high-poundage longbows.

Wood arrows are available either as completely finished products or as raw wood shafts. Traditional archery suppliers such as 3Rivers Archery, Rose City Archery, and Kustom King Traditional Archery provide everything you need to turn raw wood shafts into finished arrows, including stains, sealants, feathers, and fletching jigs to apply the feathers. They also offer finished arrows. If you're serious about wooden arrows, you can purchase raw shafts in bundles of a hundred and, for a price, the arrows can be hand spined and weighed to ensure that each one in the bundle will be matched as closely as possible to achieve consistent arrow flight.

Construction

All wooden shafts, regardless of species, begin life as a piece of lumber, roughly the size of two-by-four, and are about 36 inches long. These blanks are sawed into pieces roughly $3/4$-inch square, then passed through a doweling machine, which reduces the square piece of stock to a raw wooden shaft. The doweling machine produces shafts ranging in size from the hefty $3/8$-inch size for heavy bows down through $23/64$-inch, $11/32$-inch, and $5/16$-inch, each for progressively lighter draw weight bows.

Before a raw wood shaft becomes an arrow it goes through several steps, including hand weighing and spine testing. First, the raw shaft

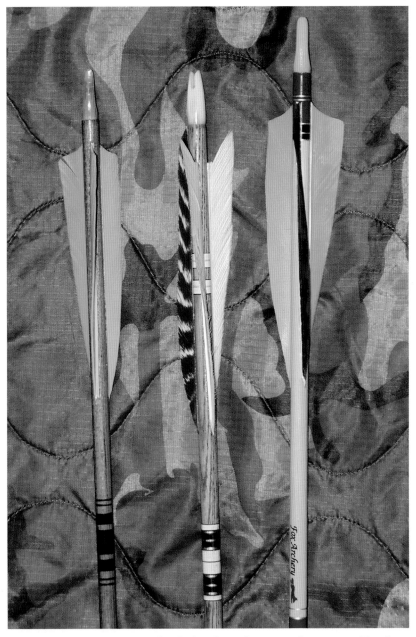

Wood arrows are one option for the longbow shooter, and many consider them to be the most traditional.

must be sanded to remove splinters and ensure a smooth finish. Some are then stained and all are given several coats of lacquer to seal and waterproof them. Wood arrows are available in either the raw state for making your own arrows from start to finish; in a finished state with the sealant already applied; or as a fletched and finished arrow.

After the shafts are made, they are cut to a length of 32 inches, examined for defects, and then readied to be sold. Generally, the shafts are sorted according to weight prior to shipping, but they may vary by as much as 40 to 50 grains. Once the shafts reach the retailer, they are weighed again and sorted into groups whose weights are much closer. Depending on the quality of shaft desired by the consumer, the shafts are weighed again to be as close as possible, then spine tested to make sure the stiffness of each arrow in the batch is as close as possible. Arrows intended for hunting have much closer tolerances, both in physical weight and spine, than "field grade" arrows used for general shooting and target practice. Obviously, the price of a set of hand-matched arrows is greater than the price of a dozen field-grade arrows, but these will produce much tighter groups when shot, if you do your job.

In order to make tougher shafts, some companies offer what are known as "compressed" shafts. Starting with a $^{23}/_{64}$-inch shaft, the dowel is spun through blocks with progressively smaller holes. The decreasing circumference makes the shaft smaller in diameter, and the heat of the friction heats up the resin in the wood and tempers the wood slightly, making the shaft both harder and stiffer.

Some longbow shooters who refuse to shoot anything but wood arrows also use footed shafts. A footed shaft is an arrow with the last several inches of the point end cut off. A section of hardwood, such as purpleheart or walnut, is joined to the arrow using a strong splice. The tougher wood at the point end prevents breaking and splintering better than the softer wood of the shaft and adds weight to the front of the arrow, helping arrow flight and aiding penetration. Footed shafts are difficult to make, and the price reflects the effort that goes into their production. They are generally only available from specialty arrow makers, although a specific internet search will reveal dealers who supply both tools and instructions for making your own footed shafts.

Wood arrows can also be tapered, with the diameter gradually decreasing toward the nock end of the arrow. If you have trouble with arrow flight, tapered arrows may help. Your problems may be a result of your shooting style, the characteristics of that particular bow, arrows that are not spined correctly, or any combination of these factors, but sometimes shooting a tapered arrow will make a huge difference because the arrows are smaller at the nock end and heavier at the point end. This enables them to straighten out more quickly than a parallel (untapered) shaft. Tapered wood is much more expensive than parallel shafting, however.

Each end of a wood arrow must be tapered to accept both the arrow nock and a field point or broadhead. The taper can either be done when the arrow is ordered from a dealer, or yourself using a special tool, much like a handheld pencil sharpener. The nock end of the arrow requires an 11-degree taper, while the point end requires a 5-degree taper. These handheld tools have two cutting blades, one for each end of the arrow. There are also tools available with a motorized sanding disk attached to a tray with both 5- and 11-degree slots, enabling you to precisely grind the taper, and a depth stop to provide the correct length of taper.

Advantages
One of the advantages of wooden arrows is that they are cheaper in

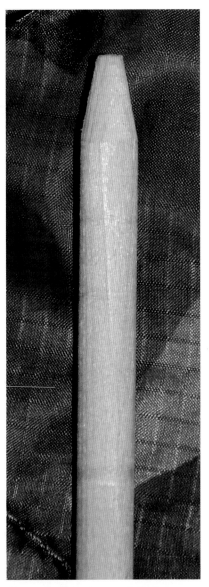

The point end of a wood shaft must be precisely tapered to 5 degrees for the field point or broadhead, and the nock end must be tapered to 11 degrees.

THE POOR MAN'S WOOD ARROW

Back in the early days of my traditional archery journey, I was on a shoestring budget and didn't have a lot of money to put into my passion for the sport. I read an article in *Traditional Bowhunter* magazine about making wooden arrows from $3/8$-inch hardware store dowel rods. The article gave instructions on what to look for, such as avoiding grain that ran off the side of the dowel, which makes it prone to break easily, and selecting the straightest ones from the bin.

So off I went to the local hardware store to peruse their bin of wood dowels of various diameters. After picking through about thirty-five to forty of the $3/8$-inch diameter ones, I found a dozen that I thought would be serviceable. One thing I noticed with nearly every dowel I picked up was that the piece was acceptably straight, except for about the last 6 inches. I'm not sure if something happened during the manufacturing process to cause this, but luckily I could cut off the crooked portion and still have plenty of length left to make my arrow.

The next major problem I ran into was that the $3/8$-inch dowel, once cut to length, was too large in diameter to fit into my taper tool. Backwoods engineering saved the day as I chucked up the dowel in a high-speed drill and wrapped a piece of rough-grit sandpaper around the other end of the dowel. With a little patience and frequent breaks to cool off my hand, I finally had both ends of the shaft down to $23/64$ inch, which fit in my taper tool.

After tapering each end, I carefully stained each shaft with several coats of walnut stain. Once that dried, I applied several coats of Minwax polyurethane finish to each shaft and allowed them to dry for several days. After gluing a nock onto the end of each shaft, I proceeded to fletch a half dozen of these dowel rod arrows, then glued on a 125-grain field point. Once I was satisfied the arrows flew correctly, the other half dozen got broadheads.

To say these arrows were heavy was the understatement of the year. I later weighed one on a certified grain scale and it was slightly more than 800 grains. But the arrows were straight and flew true, though not particularly fast, and I was ready to try one out on a whitetail.

I didn't have long to wait. One morning, early in October, a group of four large, dry does wandered under my tree stand. The closest one offered a perfect quartering-away shot, and my 65-pound recurve (yes, those were the early years) sent the arrow on its way. Whether my shot

THE POOR MAN'S WOOD ARROW

was off or the doe moved just as I released the arrow, I'll never know, but the arrow struck just in front of the hindquarter and traveled up the inside of the ribcage. The doe bounded off a few steps and stopped on unsteady legs. Within a few seconds, she began to stagger and then fell over, dead. From the time I released the arrow until the doe went down was less than fifteen seconds.

A postmortem exam showed the Zwickey broadhead had severed a large artery near the front of the ham, then traveled up through the abdominal cavity without severing anything, and cut a large slice in the liver.

This was my first experience with making my own arrows from scratch. I've found it to be a wonderful way to pass those frigid nights with the wind howling around the eaves.

If you're after a tough, heavy shaft, I recommend you make a dozen or so dowel rod arrows and see how they work for you. If you happen to own a compression block (an aluminum block with progressively smaller holes cut through it), you can use the block to compress the shafts down to $23/64$ inch, making them tougher and smaller. And, on the plus side, a dozen hardware store dowels are a whole lot cheaper than premade cedar or other hardwood arrows.

---

many cases, especially if you buy the components and build the arrows yourself. I have a few dozen wood arrows that are truly beautiful to look at. One dozen is of a more utilitarian nature, with a clear finish and fletched with wild turkey feathers. The other dozen is beautifully stained a rich dark-walnut color and sealed with a glossy finish. These arrows also feature a 10-inch crown dip in brilliant yellow, with yellow 5-inch shield-cut feathers. They're almost too beautiful to shoot and hunt with, but I do anyway because arrows are meant to be shot, not placed in a glass case and admired.

Disadvantages

There are several disadvantages to wood arrows. They have a tendency to "wander," or warp, and must be hand-straightened from time to time. This is not a difficult task for an experienced archer, but beginners may find it frustrating. Wood arrows are also affected by wet conditions and should be checked after each outing. Even the most heavily lacquered and sealed shafts will warp when exposed to water for several hours. Replacing the feathers on wood arrows can also be difficult, as you must take great care to not shave off part of the shaft when removing the arrow.

Another disadvantage of wood arrows is that they can sometimes break when shot and injure you. Once, at an IBO-sanctioned 3D archery tournament, I shot a cedar shaft that broke as I released the arrow. I never found the point of the shaft, but the nock end managed to embed itself in the back of my bow hand. After extracting it from my hand and ensuring that nothing major had been severed, I checked the rest of my cedar shafts for cracks and other deficiencies. Closer examination of the broken arrow showed that the grain of the wood, instead of extending the length of the shaft, ran off the side about a third of the way down. This produced a weak spot in the shaft that eventually led to the catastrophic failure.

It's a good idea to gently flex each wood arrow—and any other arrow, regardless of composition—prior to shooting to check the integrity and make sure you don't have an incident similar to mine, which could have been much more serious. For the record, after checking the rest of my arrows and finding them to be serviceable, I continued on and finished the tournament, but I couldn't help a mild bit of apprehension before each shot. Shortly after that, I stopped using wood arrows and switched to aluminum, even though it forced me to shoot in a different class by IBO rules.

ALUMINUM ARROWS

Aluminum arrows first saw use when Fred Bear and Howard Hill were still actively shooting and hunting. The Easton Company, better known today for aluminum baseball and softball bats than for arrows, created the process of extruding aluminum into thin tubes and turning these tubes into arrows. The process underwent several changes, as the early arrows were too stiff, heavy, or light, or bent too easily. The current standard for aluminum arrows is probably the XX75, which is offered in the Camo Hunter model, the Legacy (which has an anodized wood-grain pattern), and the Gamegetter.

Construction

Aluminum shafts are offered in different diameters with different wall thicknesses. The diameter affects arrow spine, as does the thickness of the tube wall. For example, an arrow designated as a 2315 has an outside diameter of $^{23}/_{64}$ inch, with a wall thickness of 15 thousandths of an inch. An arrow designated as a 2212 has an outside diameter of $^{22}/_{64}$ inch and a tube wall diameter of 12 thousandths of an inch. It is possible to get two different shafts with very close spine characteristics, depending on which diameter you prefer to shoot. A 2413 aluminum arrow would have nearly the same spine as a 2315, as the larger diameter makes up for the thinner tube thickness, although the 2413 would be a bit lighter in weight.

Older aluminum arrows all came with a preformed point on one end, to which the nock could be glued directly. New aluminum arrows are still available with that feature, but the trend today is for both ends of the shaft to be cut square. This allows an adapter to be glued to one end, into which a "press fit" nock is inserted, and enables you to rotate the nock in relation to the fletching to fine-tune arrow flight. This is not much of a concern to longbow

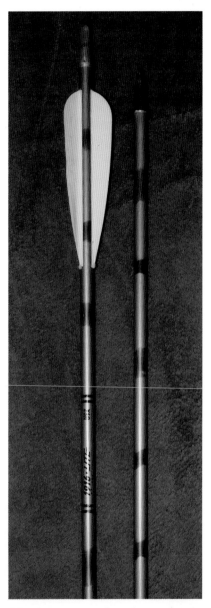

Aluminum arrows have been around for many years and offer a high degree of straightness.

shooters who shoot the arrow off the shelf, but it is for archers who shoot newer longbows that are drilled and tapped for arrow rests.

Advantages

Aluminum arrows are by nature fairly lightweight, which makes them an excellent choice if you use light draw weight longbows for target and 3D shooting. Thankfully, if you are a longbow hunter, there are methods of adding weight to an aluminum arrow to achieve the 8 or more grains of arrow weight per pound of draw weight that is so necessary for arrow penetration. The insert that the field point or broadhead screws into is threaded from the back side, allowing for as many screw-in weights as you need. There are also plastic tubes available that match the inside diameter of an aluminum shaft and can be slid inside to add overall weight to the arrow. The fit is very snug, which keeps the plastic tube from rattling around inside and has little effect on the actual stiffness of the aluminum shaft.

One of the best features of aluminum arrows is the ease with which feather fletching can be replaced. All it takes is a sharp knife to completely remove both feather and glue and make the arrow ready for a new set of feathers.

Aluminum arrows also are impervious to moisture and heat, so you never have to worry about anything rusting on your arrows, except the broadhead.

Disadvantages

One of the biggest disadvantages of aluminum arrows is that once a shaft is bent, even slightly, it's nearly impossible to straighten it out enough to make it serviceable. Considering the price of a dozen good aluminum arrows, replacing them can get expensive quickly.

CARBON ARROWS

We've now arrived at the pinnacle of arrow technology. Some may argue that carbon arrows are not "traditional" enough to shoot from a longbow. Personally, I shoot what works for me, and my quiver is always filled with carbon arrows. I look at it this way: I have fiberglass and carbon laminations in my longbows, and practically everything on earth contains carbon molecules (including the human body), so I've never had a problem with them.

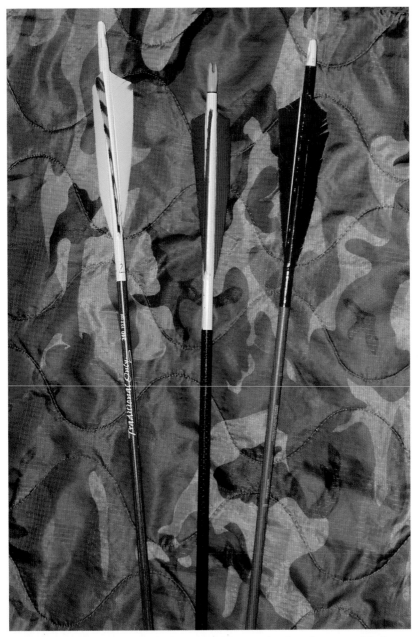

Arrows made of carbon are the most durable. I prefer them because of their toughness.

Early carbon arrows were jokingly called "soda straws" because they were about $1/8$ inch in diameter. Another disadvantage of the early models was that if you shot a game animal and the shaft broke off, carbon filaments became embedded in the meat, making it necessary to cut out a section of flesh to avoid ingesting these fibers, which obviously could cause a serious internal problem if the splinter lodged in the digestive tract. In fact, because of such occurrences this warning was printed on early carbon arrows shortly after they came on the market.

Thankfully, carbon arrow technology has grown by leaps and bounds, and splintering is no longer much of a concern. The carbons I shoot and hunt with all break off cleanly, if they break at all (which is highly unusual). There are so many advantages to carbon arrows that I can't see myself ever shooting anything else.

As a matter of fact, carbon has caught on and gained such a huge following that even Easton, the originator of the aluminum arrow, has started producing several very high-quality models of carbon arrows. Other manufacturers include Beman (who produced the first "soda straw" arrows), Gold Tip, Carbon Express, Arrow Dynamics, and Alaska Bowhunting Supply.

Construction

Alaska Bowhunting Supply, owned and operated by my good friend Ed Schlief and his son, Garrett, offers three different models of their GrizzlyStik carbon arrow: the Sitka for draw weights of 40 to 50 pounds, the Alaskan for draw weights of 50 to 80 pounds, and the Safari for draw weights of 55 to 100 pounds. They also offer a parallel model for those who don't wish to use a tapered GrizzlyStik. These arrows are able to satisfy such a wide range of draw weights because they're tapered and almost infinitely tunable so that excellent arrow flight can be achieved from any longbow. GrizzlyStiks are made from multidirectional woven carbon, which makes them extremely strong. I've used GrizzlyStiks for years and can attest to the fact that they are highly effective. It's an unusual occurrence if an arrow from my heavy longbow doesn't pass completely through the game animal, including those big, tough, corn-fed bruiser bucks I hunt here in Indiana.

Another quality carbon arrow that I have in my arsenal is made by Easton exclusively for 3Rivers Archery. With the name Traditional Only, the natural appeal for a longbow addict like me is immediately obvious.

While it has a wood-grain finish, you have to look closely to see that it isn't actually a wood arrow. The arrow is parallel, as opposed to tapered like the GrizzlyStik, but at a $5/16$-inch diameter it flies like a dart from my heavy longbows. With the added weight to the inserts, I get a finished hunting arrow that weighs more than 650 grains.

Just like the GrizzlyStik, the carbon arrows by Arrow Dynamics are also tapered. While the GrizzlyStik is a constant taper from point end to nock end, the point end of the Arrow Dynamics shaft is parallel from the point end back, with about 10 inches of the nock end tapered, just like a tapered wooden arrow. This offers the same advantages as the tapered wooden arrow in a carbon shaft, and the arrows are very high quality.

Advantages

The obvious advantage to shooting carbon arrows is the fact that they're tough as nails and impervious to moisture and heat, although I don't recommend leaving them in the sun inside a hot vehicle with the windows rolled up. A few years ago, I did a test comparison of three of the most popular carbon arrows, subjecting them to ridiculous levels of heat

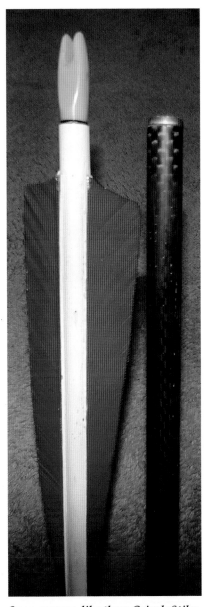

Some arrows, like these GrizzlyStiks from Alaska Bowhunting Supply, are tapered, which makes them easier to tune and helps with arrow flight.

and cold, as well as unreasonable forms of punishment like shooting them into hard targets (such as concrete blocks), just to see how tough they really were. Those tests proved to me that carbon is as close to the perfect arrow material as you can get. That's why I shoot them.

In my opinion, carbon arrows are the best option available, whether or not you hunt. They have the consistency in weight and spine of the aluminum arrow. The straightness tolerance—measured by how much the shaft deviates from perfectly straight and measured in hundredths of an inch—on my Traditional Only arrows is +/- .003 and the weight variation between shafts is +/- 2 grains. Carbon arrows also offer plenty of weight, and they're as tough as nails and can withstand a whole lot of abuse. I've glanced carbon arrows off of trees, shot them through the shoulder blades of big bucks, achieved enough penetration through the tough shoulder of a wild hog to pierce the heart, and used the same arrows over and over without problems.

Disadvantages

When picking a carbon arrow from among the dozens on the market, make sure your choice meets your needs. At least one carbon arrow on the market consists of a carbon exterior wrapped around an aluminum interior. In essence, it's an aluminum arrow inside a carbon arrow. What little experience I've had with these arrows wasn't positive. As I stated earlier, aluminum bends and stays bent. If the arrow strikes a glancing blow, the aluminum interior will bend and the carbon will stay bent at that point as well, rendering a very expensive arrow useless. The quality may have improved since I tested a few of these arrows, but be sure to do your homework if you decide that's the carbon arrow you want to shoot.

POINTS

After you've determined your arrow length, draw weight, and spine, and decided what arrow material you want to shoot, you must decide what weight broadhead or field point you want to use. For target archery or 3D shooting, a lightweight field point is advantageous because it allows the arrow to fly in a flatter trajectory. However, an arrow intended for hunting should carry a heavy field point or broadhead (see Chapter 12). Also try to choose a field point that is the same diameter as your arrow, as this will make the arrow easier to pull from the target.

A fletching jig allows longbow enthusiasts to make their own arrows with a high degree of creativity.

DO IT YOURSELF
Making your own arrows is a simple matter once you learn the basics and it will save you money in the long run. You'll need the basic components: arrow shafts, nocks, points, feathers, and a fletching jig. Remember when ordering wood shafts that about 1 inch of the point end will be tapered for the field point or broadhead. Wood arrows are measured from the bottom of the nock groove to the back of the field point or broadhead taper, while aluminum and carbon arrows are measured from the bottom of the nock groove all the way out to the end of the shaft.

Fletching Your Arrows
Replacing feathers on your arrows is something you'll need to learn to do yourself, even if you have no desire to build your own arrows, and especially if you shoot a lot like I do and your feather fletching gets

dragged through bushes, vines, and briar thickets. All you need are feathers and a fletching jig.

Often the first mistake is failing to realize that feathers come in either a left wing or right wing configuration. The clamp on every fletching jig is made to apply either a left wing or right wing feather. No clamp can do both. It makes little difference whether you shoot left wing or right wing feathers on your arrows—they both fly the same, provided the arrow is of the correct length and spine weight. Some broadheads are sharpened on a bevel, either right or left, and that's the only time you need to worry about which wing your feathers come off of. If the broadhead you've chosen has a right bevel, you should use a right wing feather. On the other side of the coin, if your single-bevel broadhead has a left bevel, you should use a left wing feather.

The actual length and profile of your feather fletching can also affect your arrow flight. Some longbow shooters who shoot thin, light arrows can get away with shooting 4-inch or even 3-inch higher-profile feathers to straighten out their arrows during flight. If you do everything with the same bow and arrows, I would recommend a feather in a length between 5 and $5\frac{1}{2}$ inches in either a parabolic (rounded at the back) or shield cut (shaped like a parabolic feather but with a slight dish-shaped cutout at the back end). Unless you're having serious arrow flight problems because of improper tuning, fletching of that size is all you need. The longer and higher the feather, the more quickly the back end of the arrow is stabilized and the quicker the arrow starts flying straight, as long as the arrow and bow are tuned to shoot together. The downside? Longer feathers with higher profiles tend to slow the arrow down, but not at the distances encountered while hunting and doing realistic target practice. Some hunters like their arrows fletched with four feathers in a 4-inch length; while it is attractive looking, I've never had the need for a fourth feather.

Flu-flu arrows are untrimmed feathers, usually 6 to 8 inches long, wrapped in a spiral around the upper end of the arrow with the express purpose of slowing the arrow down very quickly so that you can find it easier. Flu-flus are commonly used when hunting birds, rabbits, squirrels, and other small game when a missed shot would mean a long trek in search of the errant shaft. The arrow in flight, at reasonable ranges, still packs enough kinetic energy to kill small game.

One product I've found particularly useful, especially when re-fletching carbon arrows, is the vinyl arrow wrap. When using these wraps, all you need to do to remove the one already on the arrow is place the nock end into boiling water for a few seconds to soften the wrap. The vinyl wrap peels off the shaft, feathers and all. Just make sure you don't leave the end of the arrow in the boiling water for more than a few seconds, or the epoxy resin that holds the carbon fibers together will melt. These wraps also work well on both aluminum and wooden arrows. Obviously it's not beneficial to submerge the nock end of a wooden arrow in boiling water, but the judicious application of heat with either a hairdryer or heat gun will soften the arrow wrap enough that it can be removed easily.

Arrow wraps are available in a wide variety of colors, including clear, and will give your arrows a custom look without the mess and expense of paints. Unless I'm hunting wild turkeys, I tend to use brightly colored vinyl cresting wraps to help find my arrows in case I lose one in the tall grass. Remember: When hunting wild turkeys never use red, white, or blue fletching or cresting wraps because a wild turkey's head is also red, white, and blue. If you're hunting on a piece of land where there are other hunters, you run the risk of being mistaken for a wild turkey.

When replacing your fletching, the first thing you have to do is remove the old feathers. With aluminum arrows this isn't a problem. However, with wood arrows be very careful to not cut into the wood or create splinters that will affect the integrity of the shaft. Carbon arrows have an epoxy finish that is very tough, but it's still possible to damage this finish with a sharp knife. For this reason, I recommend using vinyl cresting wraps every time you fletch a carbon arrow.

Once you've removed the feathers from your wooden arrow, gently sand the areas where the feathers were previously glued, then restain and set or reseal the last 6 inches of the arrow on the nock end. For aluminum and carbon arrows, use denatured alcohol to clean the areas where the cresting wrap will be applied and allow it to dry. Next, apply the cresting wrap by laying the shaft on a soft, cushioned surface such as a mouse pad and simply rolling the cresting wrap onto the arrow shaft. After the wrap has been applied, use a clean, dry cloth to gently rub the cresting wrap in the same direction it was rolled on to eliminate any air bubbles.

Once your cresting wraps have been applied, you're ready to fletch the arrows. There are several models of fletching jigs on the market and all do a good job, but some are better than others. Fletching jigs are available either as a single fletch unit or as a multi-fletcher, which can fletch up to six arrows at once. Follow the directions that come with the fletching jig, making sure that you leave enough space between the end of the nock and where the feather starts. A good rule of thumb depending on the length and type of your nock is to allow about $5/8$ inch of space between the back end of the feather and the end of the nock to give your fingers room when you get ready to shoot. Many of the clamps that come with fletching jigs have a witness mark on them, showing where the back edge of the feather should be in the clamp. This will ensure that all of your feathers are even and an equal distance from the arrow nock. Also be careful to avoid applying too much glue to the feather or you may end up gluing the feather to the clamp, which will make it difficult to release. Most fletching cements dry fairly quickly, but I allow about twenty minutes between feathers to ensure that the glue has time to dry completely.

Mounting Points

When ordering arrows, I recommend that you order them cut to length already, unless you have a cutoff saw with a high-speed blade that allows a clean cut of both aluminum and carbon shafts. The end cut must be clean and square or the insert will not seat squarely and it will be difficult—if not impossible—to get the arrow to spin true with a broadhead or field point on the end. If the arrow doesn't spin true, it won't fly straight.

Many bowhunters believe that the blades on the broadhead need to be lined up with the feather fletching on the arrows in order for the arrow to fly straight. In other words, all three blades on a three-blade broadhead should line up with the three feathers on the arrow. However, as long as the arrow started out straight and the insert is sitting squarely inside the shaft, it doesn't make any difference how the broadhead is oriented to the feathers. When I put broadheads on my arrows, I simply screw them down tightly to make sure they don't loosen in flight, spin test them, sharpen them, and put them in my quiver. I've never had a problem with arrow flight caused by broadhead orientation as long as all of the components were properly assembled.

For mounting field points and broadheads on wooden arrows, I recommend using hot melt glue made specifically for archery applications. Before gluing on the broadhead or field point, place it firmly over the taper and spin test it. If the arrow doesn't spin true, rotate the field point or broadhead slightly and spin test it again. Many times the ferrule of the broadhead or field point isn't exactly true, which can cause difficulty when attempting to get the arrow to spin test properly. Slightly rotating the broadhead or field point will often take care of the problem.

Adding Inserts

When gluing inserts into aluminum or carbon arrows, you can use either hot melt cement, superglue, or epoxy. Just as with wooden arrows, place the insert—with the field point or broadhead already firmly screwed in—into the end of the shaft and then test the fit. Check for any looseness or wobble that will create problems when trying to get the arrow to spin true. Once you're sure the insert fits properly, spin test the arrow. If the arrow wobbles a little during the spin-testing procedure, rotate the broadhead or field point slightly and repeat the test. Once you're satisfied with the spin test, glue in the insert.

Finishing Your Arrows

The finish on carbon and aluminum arrows requires no maintenance, but it doesn't hurt to apply a coat of paste wax to wooden arrows from time to time.

Before shooting your arrows, flex each one slightly to ensure its integrity and check for any defects that may cause a failure in the arrow.

Remember, the arrow is the most important component of your archery tackle. You can scrimp a little when it comes to buying a bow and accessories, but always buy the best arrows you can afford. If you take care of them and inspect them frequently for defects and worn feathers, they should last you many seasons.

- 6 -

Shooting Accessories

Before you shoot the first arrow from your longbow, there are a few accessories that are necessary not only for accurate shooting but also for comfort and safety. The two most important ones are an arm guard and a shooting glove or shooting tab.

ARM GUARDS

The arm guard serves two purposes: It keeps your bulky sleeve out of the way of the bowstring and it protects your arm should the bowstring accidentally make contact during the shot. Generally, the brace height on many longbows is lower than the brace height on recurves, which means the bowstring is closer to the bow hand. *Brace height*, or fistmele, is the distance from the bowstring to the innermost portion of the inside of the longbow grip. A lower brace height can sometimes cause the bowstring to slap the inside of the forearm if the longbow isn't held correctly—a fairly common occurrence for beginners. All it takes to convince yourself that you need an arm guard is a single incident of the bowstring slapping the inside of your unprotected forearm. The result is both painful and obvious.

Arm guards can range in length anywhere from 6 inches up to 8 or 10 inches, covering the entire forearm, and are available in many different styles and variations. Some are made of leather and others of synthetic materials such as nylon. Arm guards are secured to the arm by elastic straps, elastic cord, or leather laces. The elastic straps on some models feature Velcro as a fastening method, and while this is handy

There is a wide variety of shooting gloves, tabs, and arm guards available for longbow shooters. Try each until you find what combination works best for you.

and allows you to quickly put on or remove the arm guard, it simply makes too much noise for a bowhunter. Another alternative is a type of long elastic cuff with thick nylon sewn in to protect the forearm. In essence, it's a tight-fitting sleeve that reaches from wrist to elbow. It's available in many colors, including camouflage for the bowhunter.

I use a couple of different arm guards, depending on the time of year and how much clothing I'm wearing. The first is for warmer weather and is made of leather. It secures with three elastic cords that loop around three bone buttons. My second arm guard is longer and covers most of the bicep on my left arm, going all the way down to the wrist. It secures with five adjustable elastic bands that fasten with a buckle.

While I believe in the saying "If you buy cheap, you get cheap," this doesn't necessarily apply to arm guards. As long as it protects your forearm and stays securely in place, that's all you need.

SHOOTING GLOVES OR TABS

You will also need a shooting glove or a tab. Choosing one or the other is a very personal decision, and I suggest trying both before making your selection. Both have their advocates, and arguments can be made for the advantages of each. Personally, I prefer a shooting glove because it allows all my fingers to move freely, and I don't have to remove it if I need to pick up something.

One of the disadvantages to using a shooting glove is that it can get hot during warm weather and make your hand sweaty, although it has never made me uncomfortable enough to switch from the glove to the tab. When a shot opportunity materializes while hunting, I don't want to have to fumble around with a shooting tab, making sure it's in the correct position before I grab the string. When I'm wearing my shooting glove, all I have to do is reach down and feel for the arrow between my first and second fingers to know I'm in the right spot.

There are several different styles of gloves available with different materials on the fingertips. One particularly good glove for those who shoot medium- and lightweight longbows is the Dura-Glove. The fingertips are covered with a soft, slick material that feels like soft felt but provides a very slick release. Other gloves have no overlays on the fingertips at all, providing a good feel for the string but little protection for the fingers if you shoot a bow with a heavy draw weight. Shooters have different preferences for how much they want to feel the string and how much (or how little) they want their hand covered. If the glove seems like your style, try as many different models as you can before settling on one particular style. Chances are you may change styles several times throughout your journey until you find the "perfect glove."

My favorite shooting glove is the Super Glove, an all-deerskin glove with cordovan leather fingertip overlays that are extremely durable, very slick, and provide plenty of protection for shooting heavy bows. Lately, I've been using a heavy-duty glove made for Kustom King Archery under the name Bearpaw. The heavy covering over the fingertips does a great job of protecting my fingers from the bowstring on my heavy, 68-pound longbow, but the leather is soft enough to allow a good sense of feel and is as comfortable as my Super Glove.

Shooting with a tab has its advantages as well. Most tabs have a "finger fender" on each side of the slot where the arrow fits, which protects the insides of the fingers and allows for a clean release. When not in use, the tab can simply be rotated to the top of the fingers, where it's out of the way and will not interfere with dexterity. Another advantage for shooting tabs is that they're generally thicker than the fingertips of a shooting glove and therefore provide more padding between the fingers and the bowstring if you shoot a longbow with a heavy draw weight.

The face of the shooting tab (the part that contacts the bowstring) is generally either leather (cordovan or cowhide) or calf hair. Calf hair produced a smooth release when I shot lighter draw weight bows, but the hair soon wore off, leaving a bald spot in the middle of the tab's face. A very good tab to try—and a style that produces a clean release—is one faced with cordovan leather (the part of the leather that comes from a horse's rump). These tabs wear extremely well, are as tough as iron, and seldom if ever develop a groove where the string sits across the face of the tab. Black Widow Custom Bows makes a particularly good model called the SuperTab, which is available in both cordovan leather and calf-hair facings.

There are also finger tabs made especially for shooting "three fingers under the nock," a style I discuss more in Chapter 8. These tabs have no slot in the middle of the tab for the arrow. Some of them also feature the "finger fender" at the top of the tab to protect the top of your index finger.

The fact is, there are more variations on shooting tabs and gloves than I can describe here. I recommend looking through traditional archery catalogs or websites, such as Kustom King Archery or 3Rivers Archery, to see what's on the market.

QUIVERS

An arrow quiver is an equally important part of your longbow gear for the obvious reason—you cannot just carry around a handful of arrows when shooting, especially while hunting. The Native Americans and every other culture around the world recognized this fact, and they came up with several ingenious methods of carrying their arrows wherever they traveled.

There are four types of arrow quivers available to the modern longbow shooter, and each has its advantages and disadvantages. Each also can be used in several different circumstances.

There is a quiver type available for every interest and purpose. I've made use of each as the situation required. Pictured here from left to right are a back quiver, a bow quiver, and a side quiver.

Back Quivers

The back quiver is the type most often associated with the longbow. Howard Hill preferred the back quiver above all others, and most old pictures of longbow hunters show them with this particular piece of equipment. Consequently, many modern-day longbow shooters prefer it as well since it's historically accurate and "just feels right" when carrying a longbow. Even with all of the new and improved quivers on the market today, the back quiver still enjoys a huge following, especially with those who like to do things the way Howard Hill did.

The back quiver, as its name implies, is worn on the back and can carry anywhere from five or six arrows up to two dozen comfortably and within easy reach of the shooter. However, drawing an arrow from the back quiver, nocking the arrow, and preparing to shoot quickly requires some practice.

MY HOMEMADE BACK QUIVER

Like many other newlyweds with a passion for bowhunting, I had a limited amount of hard currency I could sink into my "other" passion (the first being my family). Rather than spend a lot of hard-earned coin on a back quiver, which I thought I needed because Howard Hill used one, I decided to make my own from a section of thin-walled PVC pipe, about 8 inches in diameter. I cut a circular wooden plug out of plywood and fit it into one end, securing it with screws that ran through the PVC into the side of the wooden plug. I then sacrificed a leg from a pair of my old Battle Dress Uniform pants from my days as a grunt in the U.S. Army in the early eighties. I snugged it up over the tube, tucking the overhanging ends down inside the open end of the pipe and securing them with epoxy. I fastened a padded strap from some old carry-on luggage, fitted with an adjustable buckle, to the top and bottom of the PVC pipe with a short nut and bolt. Then I finished it with a 2-inch-thick piece of foam rubber in the bottom.

I used this quiver for several seasons and it worked quite well, although I did later drill some holes in the wooden plug at the bottom to allow water to drain out. I still have that quiver and now use it to store arrows that are no longer serviceable for hunting big game and have been relegated to use as small-game arrows.

Most back quivers are made of latigo leather, which is very durable and provides just the right amount of stiffness while still being supple enough to eventually mold to your back. Many quality back quivers also offer an accessory pocket built into the back part of the quiver for carrying a spare bowstring or spare shooting glove, or even lunch.

Some back quivers are made of synthetic materials. I don't recommend these for anything more than occasional backyard practice or range shooting. Depending on the quality and the amount of leather and decoration involved in the construction, you can expect to pay upward of $200 or more. Here, once again, you get what you pay for and, with reasonable care, a good back quiver will last you a lifetime.

One word of caution: A lot of archers like to deck out their back quivers with shiny medals that they've won at archery tournaments, or various other objects like deer tails or turkey feathers. That's fine if you're participating in a 3D shoot or an archery tournament, but when you're hunting, anything that makes excessive noise or reflects sunlight will alert the game to your presence.

There is also the problem of broadheads rattling around in the bottom of the quiver as you try to move quietly through the woods. Howard Hill used to fill the bottom of his back quiver with dry oats or a handful of green grass to keep the broadheads from making noise or rubbing together and dulling. If you don't like the thought of having to clean oats or dry grass out of the bottom of your back quiver, there are sheaths available that fit over each individual broadhead and secure to the arrow by a thong. These work much better than the previously mentioned alternative. Another method is to tie each broadhead sheath to the others by the thongs attached, and then place the sheaths over the broadheads before placing the arrows in the quiver. By doing this you only pull out the arrow, leaving the sheath in the quiver.

One of the greatest disadvantages of the back quiver is the difficulty of moving through thick cover such as vines and heavy brush without the arrows or the quiver getting caught in the brush. Practically the only way to avoid this is to tuck the quiver underneath your arm while moving through heavy cover.

The Catquiver, the modern version of a quiver invented by Glenn St. Charles many years ago, is also classified as a back quiver. A hunting partner of Fred Bear, St. Charles created the Pope and Young Club, which keeps track of trophy animals taken with archery tackle. His Catquiver consists of a hood that completely covers the fletching of the arrows. Two adjustable rods connect it to a wide channel where the points of the arrows go. By adjusting the distance between the top of the hood and the channel at the bottom, the arrows are held in place by pressure, with the broadhead points pressed lightly into the foam rubber of the channel and the nocks pressed lightly into the hood.

There are several versions of the Catquiver, which hold from eight to ten arrows. Each version (except the Mini-Catquiver) comes with a variety of pouches attached to the hood, allowing the quiver to serve double duty as both arrow quiver and backpack. With each progressive model, the carrying capacity and storage pouches get larger. It's a handy quiver for a daylong or two- to three-day hunt when you need to carry more than just water and a snack.

Bow Quivers

Another alternative, and one quite popular with the bowhunter, is the bow quiver. Bow quivers are available in several models and styles that hold anywhere from three to eight arrows. If your long-bow is equipped with quiver inserts, you can use a bolt-on–style quiver. There are also bow quivers that slide down over the limbs or use rubber straps to secure each part of the quiver to the upper and lower limb.

The greatest advantage of the bow quiver is that it keeps the arrows right at your fingertips. The broadheads also are protected by a foam-filled hood, which allows each broadhead to be pressed into the foam.

One problem with the bow quiver—the same as with the back quiver—is that the fletching remains unprotected. Fortunately, there are fletching covers available that will cover and protect the fletching from the elements and damage by trees and brush. If your arrows are fletched with brightly colored feathers, a camouflage fletching cover comes in handy, especially when hunting wild turkeys. These fletching covers feature a long elastic strap that can be used to hold down the cover and keep it from coming off when moving through thick brush. The

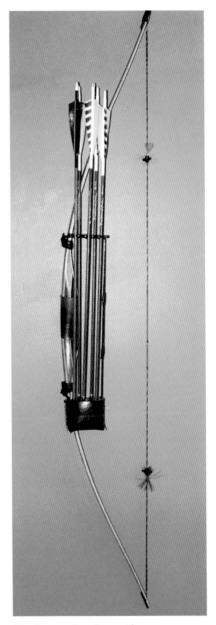

The bow quiver keeps the arrows right at your fingertips, allowing for quick follow-up shots when hunting.

fletching cover does not need to be removed to withdraw an arrow from the quiver. All you need to do is lift up slightly on the arrow to clear the broadhead from the lower part of the quiver, pull out slightly to free the arrow shaft from the gripper, and draw the arrow straight down out of the fletching cover. The arrow can be replaced in much the same way.

Some bow quivers offer the advantage of being removable, which is an asset when you're hunting from a tree stand or ground blind and don't want the added weight of the quiver on the bow. These quivers can be hung from a convenient tree limb or leaned against the edge of the ground blind, offering immediate access to the arrows should a game animal come along.

Some longbow enthusiasts don't believe that a bow quiver belongs on a longbow, claiming it adds too much weight to the longbow and affects the balance, an argument I can't refute. Personally, I use a bow quiver from time to time, depending on what kind of game I'm hunting and what the terrain itself dictates, but have never quite become accustomed to its unbalanced feeling. I'm used to the light weight of the bare longbow in my hand, and I always shoot better when there's nothing on my longbow. Recurve bows or longbows with heavier, recurve–like risers benefit more from the bow quiver than do traditional, narrow-handled longbows.

Hip Quivers

Hip quivers are very popular with the 3D archery and target-shooting community because they carry several arrows easily within reach yet don't get in the way while you're shooting. These particular hip quivers are not made to carry hunting broadheads. There are, however, several styles of hip quivers made specifically for the bowhunter that have a capacity of anywhere from five to eight broadhead-tipped arrows.

These quivers have loops that allow you to fasten them to your belt. If you are equipped with thongs, you can tie the bottom part of the quiver to your leg to keep the quiver from shifting around. Like certain bow quivers, most hip quivers can be easily taken off and secured to a convenient tree branch in your tree stand or nearby in your ground blind, where the arrows are easily accessible. A fletching cover also comes in handy with a hip quiver to help protect the fletching when moving through thick cover.

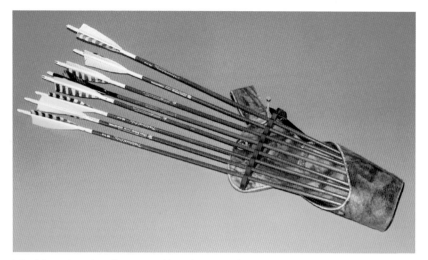

The hip quiver is a favorite of longbowmen for its utility. It can carry both field points for target shooting or broadheads for hunting, and works well if you prefer to not have a quiver mounted on your longbow.

Side Quivers

In days past, when side quivers had yet to come into their own, many bowhunters would rig their one-piece bow quiver or hip quiver with a long strap, allowing them to carry it over the shoulder in a wider variety of positions than could be used with a back quiver.

The advantage of the side quiver is that it can quickly be slung behind the back or under an arm when negotiating difficult terrain. It's also easy to remove for sitting in a ground blind. Like the hip quiver, the arrows are easily accessible and the feathers on your arrows will benefit from a fletching cover.

Certain models—particularly those made by Safari Tuff, Bow Mate, and Dawgware—are fully enclosed, protecting the entire arrow and allowing for easy, quiet removal or replacement of an arrow. These quivers feature openings near the bottom of the quiver; all you have to do to draw is reach in, grab a shaft, and lift it up and out of the opening. Some models have flaps that cover the openings, protecting the arrows from heavy downpours, and built-in compartments on the side for carrying bowhunting accessories.

The GFA side quiver is simply a one-piece bow quiver with a wool-covered broadhead cup and an adjustable strap that allows you to carry

I prefer the side quiver above all others because it can be carried in a variety of positions.

The tube quiver shown here is a cheap and effective means for carrying up to a dozen arrows with field points during practice sessions.

the quiver in a variety of configurations. G. Fred Asbell, a foremost authority on instinctive shooting with traditional bows and stalking and stillhunting game animals, designed and used this style of quiver many years ago. There is no protection for the feathers, making fletching covers a wise addition, but the quiver itself is ingeniously simple, quiet, and easy to use. I have one myself and use it for the majority of my bowhunting.

Pocket and Tube Quivers

Two other pieces of gear, although not technically considered quivers, are handy pieces of equipment that enable you to carry your target arrows while practicing without needing a full-sized quiver. The first, called a pocket quiver, is exactly that: a pocket-size and pocket-shaped piece of leather sewn to fit perfectly in your back pocket to carry field point-tipped arrows around the range. I've carried as many as six arrows in my pocket quiver without any problem, and the arrows stay secure without the worry of field points poking holes in clothing or anatomy.

The second is simply known as a tube quiver and consists of a simple leather or synthetic tube with a clip attached that allows you to carry the tube on your belt or belt loop. Tube quivers are lightweight, hold about six arrows, and are ideal for range shooting.

TARGETS

There is one last thing you really need to begin shooting your longbow. Without a target, it's extremely difficult to practice your shooting skills, unless you live on a farm with lots of round or square hay bales (or have access to some). The downside to hay or straw bales is that they don't last very long. Excelsior bales (wood shavings used by stone companies as packing between and around cut pieces of stone to protect the corners) also make excellent target bales, particularly when a frame is built that allows the bales to be compressed between two wide pieces of wood.

Bag Targets

The best target for archery practice, especially for tuning arrows and learning instinctive shooting techniques, is the bag target. Bag targets are large enough to catch all but the most errant shafts, come in a wide variety of sizes and price ranges, and last for a long time, depending on the amount of shooting you do. Bag targets are *not* waterproof, however, and I recommend storing them out of the weather when not using them. The amount of money you spend on a bag target will reflect the quality and longevity of the target. However, *don't* shoot broadheads at your bag target—they're not designed for that.

Block Targets

Most block targets are made of thin layers of compressed foam. The compression between the layers stops the arrow by creating friction on the shaft, rather than slowing the arrow down by penetration. Block targets are handy for hunting camps or for longbow shooters who don't fling many arrows. Since they're made of foam, they can be left out in the rain, although UV rays from the sun will cause deterioration over time.

The highest-quality block targets, such as those by Rinehart, are made of a solid piece of self-healing foam and will outlast layered foam targets by hundreds—if not thousands—of shots. Of course, these block targets come with a hefty price tag, but in my opinion they're worth every penny. One of the highlights of a block target? You *can* shoot broadheads at them. As a matter of fact, that's mostly what they're made for, but like anything else that gets shot repeatedly with broadheads, they will wear out and holes will form. Try to keep your broadhead shooting to a minimum—just enough to make sure they're flying the way they should prior to and during hunting seasons.

3D Targets

The 3D target is probably the most popular of all targets—and it should be, since its creation spawned a whole series of archery tournaments and competitions. These targets are made to resemble just about any animal the longbowman may hunt. White-tailed and mule deer (bucks and does), black bears and grizzlies, wild boar, mountain lion, elk, American bison—if it lives in the wild and is legitimate game, there's a 3D version of it available to shoot at. I've even shot at prairie dogs, armadillos, groundhogs, and some critters that have been extinct for a few million years.

The big names in the 3D target manufacturing business are Rinehart (the best in my opinion), Delta McKenzie, and Morrell Manufacturing. (Although Morrell is best known for its high-quality Yellow Jacket bag target, the company also offers a four-sided, layered foam broadhead target.)

3D targets vary in price, depending on how true to life the target's appearance is and what kind of foam is used. Some 3D targets come with replaceable vital zones, while others do not. I speak so highly of Rinehart targets because the foam they use to build the targets is of an unusual consistency, almost like soft rubber. My Rinehart deer target is at least five years old, has absorbed literally hundreds of heavy arrows from heavy longbows, has stood out in all kinds of weather, and still has not decayed or broken down. Shop around and see what your wallet can afford in comparison to your needs.

I prefer to use bag and 3D targets when practicing with my longbow.

Other Targets

There are also aerial targets—obviously use extreme caution if you're throwing them by hand—and smaller, ball-shaped targets that can be rolled along the ground and shot at as they move, as if shooting at a rabbit or other small game animal on the run.

There are a great many other items that you may decide you need on your journey with the longbow, but the ones mentioned in this chapter are all you really need to get started. You may find—actually you probably *will* find, as I did—that being a longbow shooter is more about the shooter and the bow than it is about any of the aftermarket gadgets so prevalent in the mainstream hunting publications.

- 7 -

Setting Up
Your Longbow

A new longbow, or even a used one if it's new to you, is like a stringed instrument. It must be tuned in order to perform the way it is intended. Tuning comes in two parts. The first is making sure that everything on the longbow is as it should be—the proper bowstring, serviceable shelf rest material, string silencers for bowhunters, and an overall inspection for excessive wear or abuse if it's a used bow. The second is making sure that the arrows you've selected to shoot from your longbow will fly properly and not fishtail (the back end whips side to side in flight) or porpoise (the back end goes up and down during flight). If you're new to instinctive shooting and the longbow, then fine-tuning arrow flight (see Chapter 10) will have to take place a little later on, after you've gained some experience shooting your bow. For right now, your primary concern is that you have a good bow that's not going to come apart on you at full draw or after the shot. I've had that happen to me, and it left a golf ball-sized bump on the top of my head.

INSPECTING YOUR LONGBOW
Even if your bow is brand new, it still requires inspection. People—including bowyers—make mistakes, and not everything fresh from the assembly line is without fault or flaw.
- **Limb tips and string grooves.** Begin by examining the limb tips and the *string grooves*, which are the grooves cut into the limb tips to hold the string in place. These are also called string nocks or nock grooves. These grooves should be an equal distance

Both laminated bows and selfbows have string grooves on each end, which hold the string in place. Most modern longbows also have reinforced tip overlays, allowing you to use bowstrings made from synthetic materials such as DynaFlight.

from the end of the *tip overlay*, the extra material glued over the tips of the limbs for added strength. If one string groove is higher or lower than the other, this puts an unequal strain on the limb itself and may have been a bowyer's attempt to get a slightly twisted limb to line up correctly. It will almost certainly guarantee excessive string wear and the definite possibility that the string loop may slip out of the groove completely at full draw, which can lead to catastrophic failure of the bow and injure you.

- **Tip overlays.** Make sure that the tip overlays are glued solidly in place with no gaps in the glue bond. The limb tips handle a huge load at full draw and even more at release because the limb tips are the only two places where the string actually touches the bow.

- **Laminations.** Next, check the laminations on the back of the bow (the side that faces away from you when the bow is shot) for any air bubbles or other signs that the epoxy used to glue on the lamination was not properly applied. Do the same for the laminations on the face of the bow. Look for any cracks in the glass laminations, especially around the arrow shelf where the shelf was cut out and the glass sanded.
- **Limbs.** Continue your inspection of the limbs, checking the fit and finish on each limb edge. You should see a glassy, smooth surface without any pits or splinters. Also carefully check the glue lines between the glass and other laminations in the limbs. Sometimes the epoxy doesn't spread all the way to the limb edge, creating a tiny crevice. Water can easily enter this crevice and over a period of time will cause delamination of the limb, another unhappy occurrence that spells the end of your shooting day.
- **Arrow shelf.** If the limb tips and limbs are okay, move on to the arrow shelf. Inspect all of the corners and edges, making sure there are no cracks or splits in the glass laminations or wood. If your bow has a leather grip on the handle, it will be impossible to check the condition of the wood under the leather unless you choose to remove it. This shouldn't be necessary unless you notice something wrong within the laminations of the handle itself.
- **Finish.** Once you've checked the bow from end to end and found it to be free of defects, take the bow into strong direct light and examine the finish. Whether matte or glossy, the finish should be uniform in thickness with no runs or drips.

CHECKING THE BOWSTRINGS

If the bow meets your satisfaction, then it's time to move on to the bowstring. If you're like me, you love the look and feel of a finely crafted longbow and can hardly pass by one without taking it down and looking at it. I keep one strung almost constantly, with a convenient supply of arrows in a hip quiver, just in case the mood strikes me to shoot a few arrows . . . and it always does. That may be the attraction of the longbow for me—its inherent beauty, graceful lines, and unseen energy, known only when the muscles are drawn tight and the bowstring is tightly anchored.

If your bow has laminated limb tips that allow for the use of mod-ern synthetic strings—and you *know* this for a fact—so much the better. If you've bought the bow used, contact the manufacturer to see if the bow is rated for a synthetic low-stretch bowstring. If you can't contact the bow maker, stick with a Dacron bowstring. The slight gain in arrow speed derived from a low-stretch synthetic string is negligible when it comes to the well-being of you and your longbow.

A new longbow comes with a new bowstring and there's usually no need to worry about its condition. If your bow is used, however, it's always a good idea to replace the bowstring prior to stringing the bow. The easiest way to do this is to measure the old string and order two replacements the same length as the one that came with your bow. Always have two (or more) in case one gets cut, breaks a strand or two, or suffers any of the many other bad things that can happen to a bow-string when you least expect it. If you hunt with your longbow, you should always carry a spare string that has already been "shot in"—that is to say, it's had a few hundred arrows shot from it, has the nocking point and string silencers already in place, and is ready to go.

Types of Bowstrings

Remember, there are two different types of bowstring: endless loop (usually made of Dacron) and Flemish. The other part of the bowstring that merits concern is the *center serving*, the spot where the arrow snaps onto the bowstring and where you grasp the bowstring to draw the bow. On Dacron strings, this center serving is generally monofila-ment, the same as fishing line, while on low-stretch strings it is made of the same synthetic braided material as the bowstring itself. This type of center serving grabs the string and stays in place better without slipping.

It's also important to note that center serving comes in different sizes, which can affect how well your arrow nock fits on the string. The arrow nock should snap on lightly. If the bow is turned over so that the arrow points toward the ground, the arrow should remain on the string and release with a light tap of the finger. An arrow nock that fits too tightly can adversely affect accuracy and cause unnecessary wear on the serving material wrapped around the center of the bowstring for added protection.

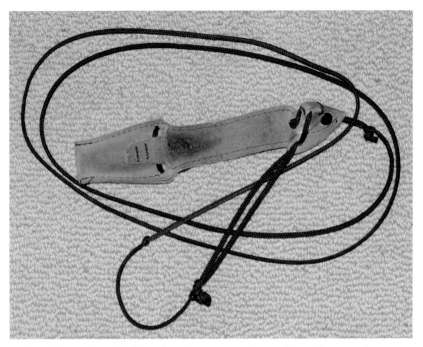

Using a bowstringer is the only safe way to string and unstring your bow. Some, like the one pictured, are made better than others. This one has a boot at each end that fits over the limp tip.

STRINGING THE LONGBOW

Once you've got your bow and string all together and you've checked to make sure everything is in working order, it's time to string your longbow. Regardless of what you've read, heard, or seen in videos, there is only *one* correct way to string your longbow and that is to use a quality bowstringer. This will prevent a limb from slipping out of your grasp and smacking you in the face or—much worse—poking you in the eye.

Bowstringers come with a boot or pocket at each end that fits over the limb tip. Begin by securing the bottom string loop into the string groove on the bottom limb. Once this is secure, place one of the boots over each limb tip and the center of the bowstringer cord under your foot. Both your feet should be positioned over the cord, slightly less than shoulder width apart, with the bow handle centered between them. By lifting up on the handle of the bow, the bow will flex, allowing you to slip the top string loop into the string groove at the upper bow

A bowstringer allows you to control the longbow during the stringing process and helps prevent damage to the longbow and injury to you.

tip. Maintain complete control of the bow during this process and be sure to *gently* lower the bow and ease pressure onto the bowstring. If you do this too quickly and one end of the bowstring isn't properly seated in the string grooves, the string will pop out and bad things can happen. By ensuring that both string loops are properly seated in their respective string grooves before lowering the bow handle, and by slowly placing pressure on the bowstring, you can avoid any surprises.

Once all pressure is off the bowstringer, remove the boots from each end. Grab the longbow by the handle and pull the string back slowly. If you hear a *pop*, this means that one of the string loops wasn't properly seated and likely slipped into place. Release pressure on the bowstring slowly. If the string should come out of the string groove, it's important to keep the bow under control.

String Silencers
If you wish to use string silencers—which I highly recommend to deaden the harmonic noise of the bowstring after the shot—some of

ALL BOWSTRINGERS ARE *NOT* CREATED EQUAL!

Nearly every new traditional bow is supplied with a bowstringer, and I've used almost all of them. The vast majority consist of an enclosed "boot" at one end of a length of heavy cord, and a rubber stopper at the other. The rubber stopper comes in many different shapes and sizes, depending on the manufacturer. The boot slips over the bottom limb tip and the stopper is positioned a little more than midway up on top of the upper limb (the closer to the limb tip, the more leverage), with the cord hanging free below the bow.

I have a lot of experience with these bowstringers, and I've had about every problem imaginable while trying to string my longbows. Usually, it's the rubber stopper that refuses to stay in place when tension is applied. Slowly, inexorably, it starts to slide up the limb toward the center of the bow, forcing you to apply extra pressure to the upper limb side in an attempt to keep the stopper from slipping. In order for the stringer to work properly, the stopper has to be placed as close to the upper limb tip as possible, but it never seems to want to stay there, and the heavier the draw weight of the bow you're trying to string, the more difficult it is to keep that stopper in place.

Thankfully, there is a simple answer. Neet Archery Products makes a foolproof bowstringer that I've used for many years with no problem. It has the normal boot on one end that fully contains the lower limb tip, but also has a smaller boot at the other end of the cord that securely contains and holds the upper limb tip. In essence, when you flex the bow to string it, equal pressure is applied to each limb tip, and it's a simple matter of slipping the upper string loop safely into the string nock. This bowstringer is not only safer and simpler to use, but also helps you keep your balance since it applies equal pressure to each bow limb during the process.

these are mounted by weaving them between sections of the bowstring. This is obviously impossible when the bow is strung. With the bow unstrung, separate the bowstring into two equal parts and place the string silencers in between at equal distances from the limb tips. You can tie these silencers in place with serving material or dental floss if you want to, but the silencers generally stay in place when the two halves of the string are brought back under tension when the bow is strung and usually don't shift.

While not absolutely necessary, string silencers deaden the sound of the bow-string at the shot and can help you hunt more successfully.

Personally, I don't like anything between the strands of my bow-string, so I use the rubber "cat whisker"–type bowstring silencers and simply tie them around the bowstring, equidistant from the limb tips. If tied tightly, they always stay in place for me. They're also very light and don't cause any loss of arrow speed, while still providing the best silencing characteristics I've found yet—and I've tried many different types of silencers. One word of caution: If your bowstring has a large diameter, such as with a heavy draw weight longbow, you may have trouble keeping the cat whiskers tied around the bowstring. In this case, it's a better idea to use floss or serving material to tie them firmly onto the bowstring, or choose another type of silencer. I've had to use

Shelf rest material covers the rest and riser of the longbow and protects them from wear. The shelf rest can be as simple as the fuzzy side of a piece of Velcro.

silencers that secure between the strands of the bowstring for one of my three main bows. I'm not happy about it, but I had no choice.

Arrow Rests

Next comes the arrow rest material. For my longbows, I use only the thin, one-piece calf-hair material with self-adhesive backing. If the bow came with rest material already applied, then there's no need to replace it unless it's worn out. Simply remove the old rest material, clean the arrow shelf and strike plate areas (the vertical part of the bow next to the shelf) on the bow handle with denatured alcohol, and reapply the one-piece shelf rest material in place of the previous one. If your bow is properly tuned, you shouldn't need to replace the shelf rest material for many months. On longbows, the thinner the shelf rest material is, the better your arrow flight will be. The rest material only needs to cover the arrow shelf and an area on the strike plate high enough to cover the sweep of the feather when an arrow is shot.

Bow Tip Protectors

Another helpful add-on, and one that I consider a must, is the bow tip protector. This is simply a rubber or plastic sleeve that fits over the lower limb tip to protect it from damage when you rest the bow on the ground. Make sure you remove the protector from time to time and clean any dirt, sand, or debris from it, as well as from the lower string loop and string grooves on the bow. Dirt and sand will eventually abrade even synthetic bowstrings, wearing through the strands and causing the string to break at the loop. A little preventative maintenance in this area will save unnecessary trouble down the line.

Nocking Points

The last thing your bow needs before it can be shot (about time, huh?) is a nocking point. The location of the nocking point is critical for really good arrow flight, but for the time being, you're just concerned about getting close. String nocks can consist of either the plastic-lined brass models that

A bow tip protector will protect the lower limb tip from damage if you rest it on the ground.

clamp around the bowstring, or just a simple piece of serving material or floss wrapped tightly around the string several times and tied off securely. Since the arrow is *always* nocked below this string nock, it will need to be higher than the arrow shelf.

If you have a bow square, you can measure the distance above the arrow shelf exactly; otherwise you can eyeball it. The bow square is a T-shaped device that clips onto the bowstring and has a scale on the

Arrow nocks keep the arrow positioned on the bowstring during the shot. They can be either the brass commercial type or simply a piece of string serving or dental floss tied around the bowstring at the correct location.

vertical arm that allows you to measure the distance between the arrow shelf and the nocking point on the bowstring. The longer horizontal portion rests on the arrow shelf and allows you to also measure brace height.

Place an arrow on the arrow shelf, slide it straight back, and snap the nock onto the bowstring. Slide the arrow nock about ¼ inch to ½ inch up the bowstring and mark the area above the arrow nock with a white crayon or a piece of tape. This is where your nocking point will be. If you're using a brass nocking point, take a pair of pliers and gently squeeze the point securely onto the string. (Nocking point pliers work best for this as they squeeze in a perfect circle, unlike a regular pair of pliers, but use what you have on hand.) It doesn't have to be torqued down so tightly that it compresses the center serving—it only needs to be tight enough that it won't move. If you're using serving material or dental floss, make several turns around the location marked on the string, then tie it securely with a couple of overhand knots. With the arrow nocked under the nocking point on the bowstring and the bow held in a vertical position, the arrow should appear to point down slightly.

Once this is accomplished, and you have your arrows, shooting glove or tab, and arm guard, you're ready to begin shooting.

- 8 -

Basic Instinctive Shooting

The two most common terms used to describe shooting a traditional bow without sights are *instinctive shooting* and *barebow shooting*. Instinctive shooting is the one most commonly used, and you'll discover as you go through the process of learning and practicing that it really is more instinctive than anything else. The process sounds very simple, but in reality it is a complex combination of focus, concentration, and muscle memory—habits that must be learned over a period of time using correct shooting form.

When shooting instinctively, your eyes see the target, focusing on the *exact* spot where you want the arrow to hit. Your eyes relay all the necessary information to your brain, which processes it and draws on the muscle memory created by thousands of shots, passing on this information to your body and telling it how high to elevate your bow arm. It's the same process that pitchers use in baseball. They look at the catcher's glove and throw at it. The body knows exactly when to release the ball because it has performed the same action countless times. Those athletes don't aim—they use their experience and muscle memory to make the ball do what they want it to do, time after time. When they miss, it's because their concentration failed.

At this point, your longbow and arrows have been set up sufficiently for you to learn the basics of correct form and instinctive shooting. Fine-tuning arrow flight will come later, once you've learned how to correctly shoot your longbow. Your longbow should be equipped with string silencers and shelf rest material. Your arrow should be equipped with field points of the weight called for by the spine chart you used during the arrow selection process. If you're a bowhunter, it's important to remember that in order to continue to experience good arrow flight, you need to use broadheads that are not only correctly designed but also of the same weight as the field points you use during the tuning process. You should also have a bag target before beginning the shooting portion of the training.

As frustrating as it may seem, you won't be shooting any arrows during the first couple of days while you're learning correct shooting form. As the old saying goes, "You must learn to crawl before you can walk." First you must begin by building your instinctive shooting foundation. The rest of your learning and experience will build on this.

ASSUMING YOUR STANCE

Your stance, or the way you address the target, is the foundation from which you build a shot. It's helpful in the beginning to have a mirror to look into as you check your stance and the way you hold the bow.

Begin by facing the target at just under a 45-degree angle. Your feet should be a little more than shoulder width apart, with the knees slightly bent. In certain circles, this position is known as the "fighting stance." Your feet should be open, with your right foot pointed in the same direction as your body and your left foot pointed slightly toward the target. (Note that these instructions are for right-handed shooters; left-handed shooters should simply reverse the directions.)

Your weight should be carried evenly across the soles of your feet, with a little extra weight centered over the thigh muscles of your front leg. This stance is solid enough that you should be able to withstand someone pushing on you from any direction without losing your balance. You should be bent slightly at the waist, with your balance centered, and your vision and concentration should be focused on the particular spot you want the arrow to hit. On a target, it might be a bull's-eye. On a game animal, it may be a tuft of lighter-colored fur or a ruffled feather. The point is you should always pick the *smallest* spot you can focus on to be your target. Stare at this spot until your peripheral vision becomes blurry and the only spot in sharp focus is exactly where you want the arrow to hit. The famous longbow trick shooter Byron Ferguson said something along the lines of if you concentrate on the spot you want to hit long enough, it becomes as big as the world, and it's impossible to miss a target that size. I'm paraphrasing here of course, but you get the idea.

Correct stance is the equivalent of the foundation of a house. A good shot is built from the ground up.

With the longbow held firmly in your bow hand and your shooting glove or tab on your shooting hand, bring the bow hand up to shoulder level and tilt the bow to the right until you can look across your bow hand with both eyes. Your bow arm should be slightly bent at the elbow, your shoulder locked solidly in place, and your grip firm on the bow. It's important not to grip the bow too tightly because this will cause torque and affect arrow flight. It's also important, for obvious reasons, not to grip the bow too loosely. A firm grip, like a firm handshake, is all that's needed.

Correct shooting form must be used on every shot in order to obtain consistent accuracy.

PRACTICING THE DRAW

Without placing an arrow on the string, position the first three fingers of your shooting hand on the bowstring, either with your first three fingers under the nock, or with your index finger above the nocking point and your middle and ring fingers below the nock. Without releasing the bowstring, hold the bow arm steady and draw the bowstring straight back, anchoring your middle finger in the corner of your mouth; then slowly allow the bowstring to pull the drawing hand back forward. You should be able to hold at full draw for several seconds without shaking. If you cannot draw the string straight back, or if you cannot hold the string at anchor for more than four or five seconds without shaking, then you're probably trying to draw too much weight. Your options here are to continue with this exercise until you can come smoothly to full draw, anchor, and hold for several seconds without shaking; obtain a bow with a lower draw weight; or use a device designed specifically to strengthen the muscles used for drawing the bow. A Bowfit device is the perfect tool for strengthening these seldom-used muscles and is available from many traditional archery suppliers.

Many archers mistakenly use their arm muscles to draw the bow. This is incorrect. The muscles used when drawing your longbow are the large muscles located between your shoulder blades. To get an idea of what I'm talking about, interlock the fingers of both hands and bring

the forearms up to shoulder level, parallel to the ground. Then, pull your hands apart and push your elbows straight back parallel to the ground. You should be able to feel the muscles between your shoulder blades doing the work of pulling your elbows back. These are the same muscles used to draw your longbow. This technique, known as "back tension," is key to accurate, consistent shooting.

When at full draw, the arrow shelf, your anchor point, the elbow of your drawing arm, and your back shoulder should all be in a straight line. If they are not, this will produce torque in either the bow hand or the drawing hand and will affect your release and the flight of the arrow. It's especially useful here to have either a full-length mirror to look into or a friend to watch you draw the bow to make sure that you are doing it correctly. Your head and chin should be tucked down close to the shoulder of the drawing arm, as this will center the arrow underneath your line of sight.

While at full draw, pay attention to your stance and maintain your balance. Make sure you control the bowstring as you slowly release it. Also keep the bow tilted slightly so that you can clearly see your target with both eyes. Continue with this exercise until you are able to perform it correctly every time. After a short rest, you can do a few more repetitions for as long as your strength holds out. If this is your first experience with traditional bows, you may find that you have sore muscles the next day. That's to be expected because the muscles used

when drawing a traditional bow are rarely used for anything else. The key here is to not overdo it and to avoid injuring yourself, which will set your progress back severely.

Continue with this exercise for several days, or for as long as it takes to feel comfortable coming to full draw and anchoring the bow-string. Again, do not rush through this practice, because your stance, draw, and anchor are all essential parts of instinctive shooting. Don't consider moving on to the next step until you've done the draw-and-anchor exercise at least five hundred times, preferably more. I simply cannot overemphasize how important these beginning steps are to your success later. Don't take shortcuts or cheat yourself—you'll only limit your potential as a longbow shooter. If you start out with incorrect shooting form or develop bad habits, you will have to go back and correct the flaws, and it will take much longer to achieve the muscle memory necessary for consistent accuracy.

SHOOTING THE FIRST ARROWS

Shooting and hunting with the longbow is my passion. I shoot every day, rain or shine, indoors and out. I usually have one longbow strung at all times with arrows, an arm guard, and a shooting glove nearby. On most days I shoot between two hundred and three hundred arrows. If you're just starting out, I would recommend that you shoot no more than a dozen, simply because at this point in time you're still building correct shooting form and are only worried about the arrows impacting somewhere in the target. Accuracy will come later.

Start by hanging your bag target at chest level, which will allow you to shoot straight into it without having to bend at the waist. Check your surroundings and the area behind your target, and conduct this exercise in the safest manner possible. Remember, once you release an arrow, you can't call it back. Safety first!

If you haven't already, it's time to make the decision as to whether you will be shooting your bow with *three fingers under* or *split fingered*. When shooting three fingers under the nock, place the first three fingers underneath the arrow nock on the bowstring. This elevates the arrow a little higher and brings it closer to your line of vision. When shooting with split fingers, the index finger goes on top of the arrow nock and the middle and ring fingers go below the nock. Take care to apply equal pressure across all three fingers to avoid unnecessary torque on the arrow. If you don't have any experience shooting a traditional bow, I suggest shooting a few arrows using both techniques to find out which works better for you, is more comfortable, and allows for the greatest accuracy.

Your first arrows will be fired from a distance of no more than four or five paces, just far enough away that once the arrow clears the bow it will immediately impact in the target. Begin by nocking an arrow, with the nock placed *underneath* the nocking point on the bowstring. Place

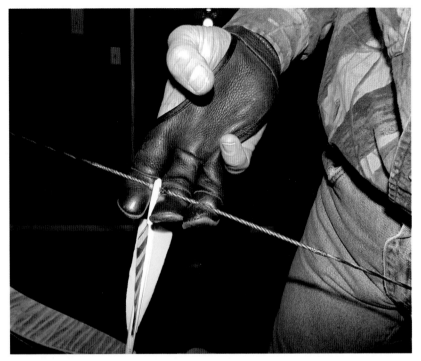

By placing the bowstring in the first joint of the fingers as opposed to using the fingertips, more strength is available to the hand during the draw. This technique is known as a "deep hook."

the first three fingers of your drawing hand on the bowstring (either three fingers under or split fingered), with the bowstring crossing the first joints of all three fingers. This is also sometimes known as a "deep hook." Some archers prefer to position the bowstring as close to their fingertips as possible to help them release it smoothly. If you are shooting a longbow with a very light draw weight, this may not create a problem. However, if you're shooting a bow of more than 45 pounds in draw weight, the bowstring may accidentally slip off your fingers as you draw. That's why I advocate locating the bowstring in the first joints of all three fingers.

Bring the longbow up to shoulder level and point the arrow at the target. Just as you did when practicing, draw the arrow straight back to your anchor point, keeping it pointed at the target, and then allow the bowstring to slip easily from your fingers. How smoothly you release

SHOOTING UPHILL OR DOWNHILL

One mistake many longbow shooters make occurs when they're shooting uphill or downhill. The tendency is to either lower the bow when shooting downhill or to raise the bow arm when shooting uphill, without shifting the position of the body from the waist up. While most shooters don't use any kind of sighting system on the bow, it would be accurate to compare the bow hand or arm and the anchor point to the front and rear sights on a rifle, respectively. If one of those rifle sights is loose, the bullet will not impact in the same location on every shot. The same applies with your bow hand or arm and anchor point. In order to shoot accurately, your eye must be in line with both sights.

Whether you're shooting a longbow uphill or downhill, you must maintain the same shooting form from the waist up—your bow hand, the forearm of your drawing hand, and your anchor point must be in line at all times. Therefore, it's necessary to bend at the waist when shooting uphill or downhill. The torso remains in exactly the same position, in correct alignment to prevent torque on the bow. This is extremely important to bowhunters who shoot from tree stands. Many times they simply drop the bow arm instead of bending at the waist. This causes misalignment of the sight picture, and the shot will usually fly too high as a result of the natural tendency to raise the back elbow. The same applies for shooting uphill. Simply bend backward at the waist and maintain your alignment. Think of your body above the waist as being locked in and immovable.

Another common occurrence when shooting up or downhill, even with correct body position and form, is that the arrow will still tend to fly too high. On shots like these, depending on the severity of the grade, always aim low. Practice these shots regularly to get a feel for how low you need to shoot to hit the mark.

the arrow will directly affect how the arrow leaves the bow and flies to the target. When you release the bowstring, your drawing hand should come straight back.

Once again, back tension is the key factor here. As you draw the bow, you should feel the muscles between your shoulder blades—primarily on the right side—pulling the bowstring back. When you anchor, continue to pull straight back until your fingers slip off the bowstring. This technique may seem difficult at first, especially for compound bow shooters, but is essential for shooting a longbow.

Remember: It's important to never overdo it. If you get tired, take a break. When you can no longer use good form, put the bow away for a day. The hardest thing in the world is to stop shooting, especially when you have a great love for it, but any injury will cost you more than a day to heal. This is a learning process, and the effort and patience you put into it will be rewarded with greater shooting skills.

Shooting with Your Eyes Closed

If you really want to develop and ingrain your muscle memory, change things up after a couple of weeks and shoot at the bag target with your eyes closed. I do this fairly often as a way to internalize my form and "feel" that everything is clicking and the wheels are turning smoothly.

Simply get close enough to the bag target so that as soon as you release the arrow it will hit the target. Once again, you're not worried about accuracy here; hitting the bag for safety's sake is all that matters. You're *feeling* what good shooting form is without the outside distraction of visual sensory input. Feel the bowstring as you put tension on it. Feel the tension in your back muscles as you draw the bowstring. Feel your middle finger touch the anchor point. Feel your back muscles continue to contract as the bowstring slips smoothly from your fingers. In my opinion, this is one of the best exercises you can use for building that all-important foundation of correct shooting form.

- 9 -

Basic Accuracy Exercises

Now that you've got your shooting form firmly ingrained and can do it right every time without conscious thought, it's time to start training your mind and body to make that arrow go where you want it to. Always keep at the forefront of your mind that your accuracy depends on your ability to repeat your shooting form shot after shot.

If your bow arm or hand is unsteady or your anchor point changes from shot to shot, it's impossible to shoot accurately. The key factor that affects steadiness—and the problem that occurs more frequently than any other—is trying to shoot a bow that has too much draw weight. Once again, if you can't draw your bow straight back to anchor and hold it there for several seconds, either build up your strength until you can draw the bow properly or get a bow that's lighter in draw weight.

TRAINING

You're going to begin this phase of practice only slightly farther away from the target than in the previous chapter. For consistency's sake, let's begin at 5 yards (15 feet). Use known distances here so that you'll have a benchmark to use each time you increase the distance to the target. This distance is close enough to ensure that you'll hit the target and far enough away to force you to focus on a spot to hit.

Keep in mind that the instinctive shooter doesn't care exactly how many yards it is to the target. In fact, you don't need to know at all because your bow arm elevation will be calculated by your brain. Remember how I described the process earlier? Your eyes see the target and your brain calculates the amount of bow arm elevation needed to carry the arrow to the target. The left and right alignment will be the

The shooter should be able to draw their longbow straight back without having to point it up or down. If you can't draw the bow straight back, chances are, you're trying to shoot a bow with too much draw weight!

easiest because your shooting form will make sure that the arrow is lined up correctly in the horizontal plane.

You will also be shooting only one arrow at a time during this phase to avoid breaking arrows and to give you plenty of time between shots to refocus your concentration. You will also have to overcome the desire to hurry your shots here. Make each arrow the most important one you'll ever shoot, and use the most focus and concentration you can summon on each shot.

Begin with the target still about chest high and make a circle about 2 inches in diameter right in the middle of it, using a piece of tape or a colored marker that contrasts highly with the color of the bag target. Making the target so small forces you to concentrate harder on focus. Step back about 5 yards and "address the target," or take up your shooting stance, and bring up your bow arm. I highly recommend drawing the bow straight back as opposed to pointing the bow down and drawing as your bring it up on target, or pointing the bow at the sky and drawing as you bring the bow down. For target shooters, this is

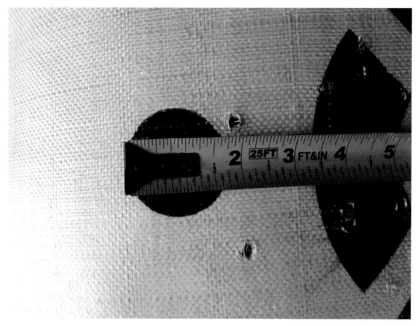

Make a circle 2 inches in diameter on the face of your bag target.

simply economy of movement; for bowhunters, drawing straight back creates much less motion that could spook game.

Before bringing the bow up, focus on the 2-inch circle in the center of the bag target until your peripheral vision is blurry. Once you've achieved this focus, bring the bow up, draw and anchor (making sure to tuck your head and chin down to align the arrow with your line of sight), continue to focus on the target spot, and allow the bowstring to slip from your fingers. Once you've released the arrow, your bow arm should stay on target until the arrow impacts.

Since you're so close to the target, chances are the arrow hit fairly close to the circle. If you're shooting with good form, it will only take small adjustments to correct the point of impact. It's very important to remember that the human brain likes order and equality. Your brain wants the arrow to go into the 2-inch circle as badly as the rest of you, simply because it appeals to your sense of order. If you have any doubts, just try this little experiment: Make a circle with your thumb and forefinger—the "okay" sign—and look at any small object through it. Notice how the eye automatically places this small object at the center of the circle? Your brain and muscles, over a period of time, will learn what needs to be done to place the arrow in the middle of what you're focusing on. The key is to be able to focus and pick a spot, and then to concentrate on that spot to the exclusion of all else.

During this exercise, only shoot one arrow at the target at a time. Once you've shot, walk up and pull the arrow. I realize that shooting only one arrow at a time is frustrating when you have a full quiver, but shooting that single arrow—and doing it as though your life depends on it—will not only help your concentration but also lessen the chance of developing a bad habit or flaw in your shooting form. When shooting several arrows at a time, you often start to hurry and don't pay meticulous attention to shooting form.

For the purposes of this exercise, you should shoot at least seven hundred arrows. Once you're hitting the 2-inch circle nine out of ten times, you're comfortable and confident in your shooting form, and you've shot at least seven hundred arrows, then move back another 5 yards. You'll see that at this distance the bag target itself appears smaller, not to mention the 2-inch circle! From this point on, you'll begin to understand how important it is to focus and concentrate on the exact spot you want your arrow to impact. I simply cannot stress this enough. Once you've trained yourself to that level of focus, your accuracy will improve dramatically as well.

At 10 yards (30 feet), you're going to follow the same practice routine as before. Shoot one arrow at a time, giving each shot the concentration needed to hit the circle, and take your time. Repetition is the key to building muscle memory and creating an encyclopedia of shots in your brain. Your brain catalogs every shot you make and calls on that information from previous times to tell your body how high to elevate the bow arm to hit the bull's-eye. The more good information your brain stores, the better you will shoot. Once you've shot at least seven hundred arrows and you're keeping the arrow in the circle nine out of ten times, move back 5 more yards.

Do the same routine again at 15 yards (45 feet), except make the circle 4 inches in diameter so that it's easier to see. You can also shoot two arrows at a time if you wish to do so. Just remember to keep your concentration at a peak level for each shot. The same rules apply: No cheating, shoot at least seven hundred arrows, and don't move back until you can keep nine out of ten arrows in the 4-inch circle.

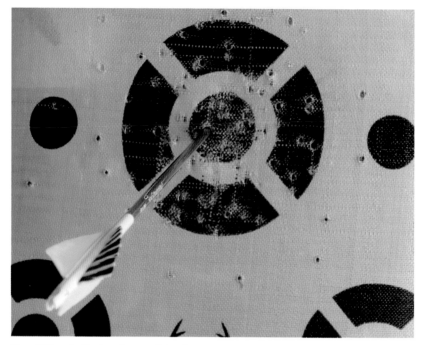

Repetition is the key to consistent accuracy.

The final stage is at 20 yards (60 feet), with all the same standards as the 15-yard exercise. You've no doubt noticed that the farther away from the target you get, the harder you have to concentrate to focus on that circle because there's a bit more "clutter" in your peripheral vision as you move back. Give each and every arrow your full attention, and keep up that good shooting form. Once you've shot at least seven hundred arrows from this distance, and you can keep nine out of ten arrows in the 4-inch circle, all that remains is to continue shooting and building confidence in your longbow and yourself.

COMMON MISTAKES

Shooting a longbow instinctively takes practice, and lots of it. During the initial learning process, you're going to be tempted to ignore what your mind and body are telling you—namely that you're either too tired to continue in a constructive manner or that your concentration is beginning to wander. Either of these conditions is a serious detriment to your learning process. Shooting a longbow is extremely enjoyable, and it should be. But just as Rome wasn't built in a day, neither will your instinctive shooting skills be. To shoot instinctively—and to do so accurately—requires a very high degree of concentration in several areas simultaneously.

Before beginning your shooting session, try to rid your mind of any worries or concerns that will affect your concentration. Sit down for a few minutes and relax. Think about what you're getting ready to do. Close your eyes and visualize your arrow impacting the center of the circle. Mentally feel the bowstring's tension against your fingers and the muscles between your shoulders tightening as you draw. When your concentration begins to falter, so will your correct shooting form and, in turn, your accuracy. It's far better to shoot six or eight arrows using perfect form than to shoot six dozen arrows without it.

There are a few common signs that it's time to put the bow down for a while and rest.

- **Distraction or worry.** If you have something on your mind that prevents you from giving full concentration to your practice session, postpone the session for later, or even for another day. You can't concentrate fully when you're worried about something.
- **Rushing the shot.** You will develop your own shooting rhythm as you learn. Rushing the shot can become a habit that will rob you of both accuracy and confidence. It can also mean you're tired and won't be able to remain at full draw as long as is necessary.
- **Short drawing.** Not coming to full draw is another sign of being tired.
- **Dropping the bow arm.** Your bow arm should remain pointed at the target until the arrow impacts. If you're dropping it immediately after the shot, it's time to take a break.
- **Raising your head.** Just like your bow arm should remain still, your head should stay down until the arrow hits the mark. If you raise your head to see where the arrow hits, or even before the arrow is released, it will obviously affect your accuracy.
- **Frustration.** This is a common problem for beginners when their arrows don't always go where they want. It's important to remember that if your bow and arrows are properly tuned, the problem lies with your shooting form. In most cases, when frustration sets in it's time to quit for the day.

- **Skipping ahead.** Many times you will become bored with the repetitive nature of the early training exercises and want to skip ahead to something that's more fun. If you're serious about the longbow and learning to shoot it, you'll understand that the process takes time and patience now that will be rewarded later.
- **Physical tiredness.** If you're too tired to shoot, you run the risk of developing bad habits. If you get tired while shooting and it becomes hard to draw your longbow, take a break.

MAXIMUM EFFECTIVE RANGE

By this point you should be very familiar with how it feels at full draw when you do it right and with how a good release feels. Now, start mixing up your distances to the target. Shoot one arrow from 5 yards, one from 20, one from 15, and so on. You can also continue to increase your shooting distance past 20 yards using the same routine as before, once you're consistently accurate out to that range. Eventually, you will reach a point from which you can no longer shoot accurately and consistently. The farthest distance at which you can consistently shoot five out of six arrows into a paper plate is your *maximum effective range*.

GAP SHOOTING

Howard Hill used the *gap shooting* method of aiming, which he called "split vision." Essentially, gap shooting involves using the point of the arrow as an aiming point and requires the shooter to know the distance to the target, much like a compound bow shooter using a peep sight and sight pins. Imagine yourself at full draw, with the arrow lined up under your eye and the tip pointed at the target. The point is held either above or below the spot where you want the arrow to strike. Your horizontal plane is set but the vertical plane, or how far up or down you need to shift the arrow, depends on your distance from the target.

Start at 10 yards (30 feet) and, at full draw, point the tip of your arrow 12 inches below the spot you wish to hit on the target. If you shoot under that spot on the target, you'll know that you need to aim less than 12 inches low. The closer you are to the target, the greater the distance between the point of the arrow and the intended point of impact. For instance, if you are 20 yards (60 feet) from the target, the point of aim for the tip of your arrow at full draw might be 12 inches below the intended point of impact. If you are 40 yards (80 feet) from the target, the point of the arrow may be 6 inches above the intended point of impact. The distance will obviously be different for every shooter because of the differences in draw weight, arrow weight, and so on. At farther distances, you will actually have to hold the point of your arrow above the target to hit the mark.

Once you learn the correct amount of gap for whatever distance you are from the target, it simply becomes a matter of holding the correct distance above or below the target to make an accurate shot. There is a certain distance from the target at which, when you put the point of your arrow directly *on* (not above or below) the spot you want to hit, the arrow will impact exactly where the tip was pointing. This is known as the *point of aim.*

While this is a very accurate way of shooting the longbow, it has obvious drawbacks. Gap shooting requires long hours of practice to learn the correct gap for any given distance, and you must be very good at judging distances and knowing how far you are from the target, something that is unnecessary when shooting instinctively. Also, unless the bow-and-arrow combination shoots an arrow with a flat trajectory, the gap between the point of the arrow and the point of impact may be measured in feet rather than in inches.

- 10 -

Fine-Tuning Your Longbow and Arrows

Now that you have correct shooting form ingrained in your muscle memory, and you're consistently accurate in your shooting, it's time to fine-tune your longbow and arrows. This fine-tuning will not only increase your accuracy but also help when shooting in a "pressure" situation, such as at a game animal or a 3D target while your buddies watch. If you've completed all of your training routines and can consistently hit what you're shooting at, then it's time to up your game.

I believe that a properly designed longbow is the most accurate traditional bow there is. There are any number of bowyers out there who will argue the point, stating that the recurve is the most accurate and easiest to shoot, but those folks generally have something to sell (such as their own brand of bow). Having shot every kind of traditional bow there is, from several excellent bowyers, I have found that longbows not only suit my shooting and hunting style better than anything else but also fit my mindset. I've always enjoyed "doing more with less," wringing every bit of performance possible out of my longbows and arrows.

I shoot every day—rain, sun, snow, or wind—and hunt in the same conditions. My longbows take a beating from the elements and time spent in the woods, and it's imperative that they be tuned to the utmost of my ability. I say "my ability" because my bows are capable of shooting a lot more accurately than I have the ability to shoot them. As I've said before, longbows are more forgiving of mistakes in shooting form than any other traditional bow. You may ask yourself: "Why fine-tune my longbow and arrows if the bow is so naturally forgiving?" The answer is simple: because you'll never know what kind of accuracy your bow is capable of if you don't. Just like finding your own instinctive shooting potential, you need to help the bow find its own.

Another key point to remember is that in order for your longbow to make use of all the energy stored in the limbs, it's important to shoot as heavy an arrow as you can, within reason. The rule of thumb is that your arrow should weigh *no less* than 8 grains per pound of draw weight. In other words, if the draw weight of your longbow is 50 pounds, your arrow should weigh *at least* 400 grains. This makes your bow more efficient and helps avoid undue stress on the limbs. Shooting arrows that are too light is nearly as bad as dry firing your bow (shooting your bow without an arrow on the string). My longbows pull between 66 and 68 pounds in draw weight, and my arrows weigh around 700 grains. That's right around 10 grains of arrow weight per pound of bow weight. I don't notice any loss of cast or shooting distance, and my accuracy is not affected in the least.

A heavy point on the end of your arrow also allows more weight front-of-center (FOC) on the arrow. FOC is a term that has only recently become a buzzword for the compound crowd, but we traditionalists have known about its advantages for a long time. A high FOC helps stabilize the arrow in flight and adds dramatically to arrow penetration in game animals.

BARE SHAFT TUNING

There are almost as many opponents of bare shaft tuning as there are proponents. Some claim the process is an unnecessary waste of time and effort and doesn't make the bow shoot any better. I strongly disagree. This tuning method helps you realize how important correct shooting form truly is and what a wonderful instrument a well-made longbow is.

The whole purpose of bare shaft tuning is to get your arrow to fly reasonably straight to the target *without feathers*. I see you shaking your head, but believe me, it is possible, and it's not very hard.

Once again, you'll need a bag target, and also one arrow with the feather fletching completely removed. Your goal is to make adjustments to the arrow itself in order to make it fly as straight as possible to the target and stick in the target at a reasonably straight angle. It helps to have someone stand behind you and watch the arrow as it flies in order

For bare shaft tuning, use an arrow without feathers and the same weight field point as the broadhead you'll be using.

to determine what it's doing that will require correction. If you have a video camera, that's even better.

The first thing you need to do is to move your nocking point up the bowstring about ½ inch. The reason for this will be obvious a little later. What you're looking for with each arrow is whether the nock end is flying to the left or right of the point end, and how the arrow is oriented in the soft bag target when it sticks. You're also looking to see if the nock end of the arrow flies higher than the point end—it will in the beginning because you've purposefully set the nocking point too high. You can see why correct form is necessary when doing this, because any mistake you introduce can be mistaken for a tuning error.

When most of us shoot the longbow, we tilt or cant the bow to one side so we can look over the arrow. When bare shaft tuning, however, we want the bow to be as vertical as possible so that we can positively identify whether the arrow is flying "nock high," "nock right," or "nock left." Shoot your bare shaft several times, beginning up close to the target in case the arrow takes off on a tangent. Try to work your way back to 20 yards (60 feet) if possible, as this will allow you

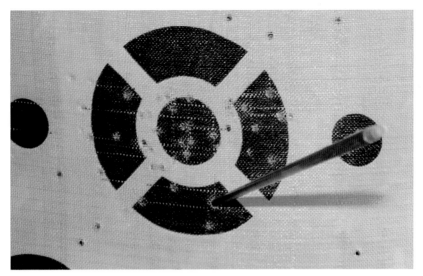

If the bare shaft impacts in the target with the nock end to the right, that means the arrow is too stiff. To correct this problem, you have to use a heavier point.

more time to watch the arrow in flight and get a better idea of how it's flying. Once you've identified how the arrow is flying (consistently nock right or nock left), it's time to correct it. (Remember the arrow is going to fly nock high because you've purposefully set the nocking point higher on the bowstring. You'll correct this anomaly last of all.)

Nock Right

If your arrow is flying with the nock end of the arrow to the right of the point end and sticks in the target that way, then your arrow has too much spine, or is too stiff. The only thing you can do is use progressively heavier field points or weighted inserts until the arrow straightens out. Arrow manufacturers have gone to great lengths to help us tune our arrows by creating weights that screw into the back of the insert that goes in the front of the shaft. Many times it's not even necessary to change field point or broadhead weights, as enough weight can be added to the back of the insert to correct nock right arrow flight.

If you don't want to add extra weight to the point end of your arrow, then your only other option is to go to an arrow with a lighter spine, or less stiffness. Spine charts are not always exact and are only

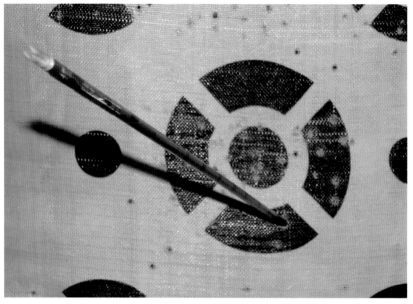

When the bare shaft impacts in the target with the nock end to the left, this means the arrow is not stiff enough.

meant to give a starting point in helping you choose a shaft of the correct spine. Many variables come into play, such as the weight and thickness of the bowstring, the efficiency of the bow, or even the weight of the string silencers. That's why it's important to tune your bow with everything that will be on it when you shoot.

Nock Left
If the arrow is flying with the nock end to the left of the point end and sticks in the target like that, then your arrow doesn't have enough spine, or is not stiff enough. This is much easier to correct than having an arrow that's too stiff. Simply remove the insert from the point end of the arrow, cut ¼ inch off the point end of the shaft, and glue the insert back in. You can continue to shorten the arrow until it either starts to fly and stick in the target reasonably straight, or until you can't cut any more off the arrow. Generally, it doesn't require much shaft removal to get your arrow flying straight. Remember your arrows should be cut at least 2 inches longer than your draw length to start with, so you have some room to work with here.

When the arrow impacts in the target fairly straight, then you can begin to move the nocking point down the bowstring until the arrow sticks fairly straight in the target in all planes.

Your only other options are to use a point with a lighter grain weight (keeping in mind the rule of thumb for total arrow weight) or to go to a shaft with a stiffer spine rating. You can also add weight to the nock end of the arrow using special nock adapters that accept screw-in weights. By adding weight to the nock end, it decreases the dynamic spine of the arrow as well as your FOC.

Nock High

Once you've got your arrow flying relatively straight to the target in the left and right planes, it's time to lower your nocking point to take care of the nock high situation. Move the nocking point on the bowstring down in small increments (about $1/8$ inch at a time) until the bare shaft starts sticking in the target in a relatively straight manner. Be careful not to move your nocking point down too far because it could cause the shaft to glance off the arrow shelf and make the arrow appear to still be flying nock high. Gradually move it down until you see the worst of the nock high flight become less. At that point, clinch the nock down tight to complete the bare shaft tuning process.

Now, when your arrows are fletched with feathers, you should see a marked improvement in your arrow flight. Using a bow square, record the distance from the nocking point to the arrow shelf and write it down for future reference so that you won't have to go through the whole process again.

BRACE HEIGHT

Various manufacturers will have different recommended brace heights for their bowstrings, usually covering about $1/2$ inch. For example, the recommended brace height for my Fox Archery longbow is from $6\frac{3}{4}$ inches to $7\frac{1}{4}$ inches, while the recommended brace height on my TimberHawk Falcon longbow is from 7 to $7\frac{1}{2}$ inches. The "sweet spot," or height where your bow is most efficient and shoots best, is somewhere between these two measurements. Consult your owner's manual for the recommended range of brace heights. If you don't have an owner's manual, try to contact the bowyer. They're usually more than happy to answer any questions you may have about your longbow.

With a lower brace height, the arrow stays on the string longer and can sometimes magnify any errors in your release. It also allows the arrow to absorb more of the bow's energy by the sheer fact that it does stay on the string longer. On the other hand, a higher brace height releases the arrow from the string a little more quickly and can help negate problems caused by a bad release. The arrow absorbs a fraction less of the limb's stored energy, but the amount is negligible and not something to worry about.

Brace height is adjusted by either twisting or untwisting the bowstring. With endless loop strings, where each string loop is served, twisting or untwisting the string has no effect on the integrity of the bowstring. But with a Flemish–type twisted string, it is possible to untwist the string to the point where the end loops will separate. Use caution here, as a Flemish string that lets go can cause catastrophic failure to the bow and possibly injure you.

Experiment by shooting your bow set at different brace heights and recording which seems to produce the best arrow flight from your bow.

GETTING TO KNOW YOUR EQUIPMENT

Howard Hill was the most famous longbow shooter of his day and performed feats with his longbow that amazed thousands of people. Since spine testers had not yet been invented, he came up with a unique way of determining how his arrows flew from his heavy longbow. After making a batch of two to three dozen arrows, Hill would take them out behind his shop where he had a pile of sand for target practice. Using an empty butter carton or some other small target, Hill would shoot each of the arrows. The ones that hit the target would be gathered up and secured with a rubber band. The ones that hit to the left of the target would be banded together and marked, and the same with those that hit to the right of the target. Whenever he shot one of the arrows from the latter two groups, he would know he needed to aim to the right or to the left to compensate and hit the target. That was spine testing the Howard Hill way.

Hill also loved shooting in archery competitions and, as the world's greatest archer, was frequently called upon for impromptu archery exhibitions with his longbow. One of Hill's favorite demonstrations was to go around to several members of his audience and take one or two of their arrows. It didn't matter how long or short the arrows were, or whether they were spined to shoot from a 20-pound target bow or an 80-pound hunting bow. He would then station himself 30 yards (90 feet) from a target and proceed to shoot every arrow into the dead center of the target. For the short, light arrows, he would pull his heavy bow back only a few inches. He had a feel for the bow and arrow developed over a lifetime of shooting and hunting with the longbow, and truly deserved the title of "The World's Greatest Archer."

Byron Ferguson, whom some call the "Modern-Day Howard Hill," has performed many of the same amazing shots that Hill did in his day. Ferguson attributes his uncanny accuracy to lots of practice and, even more importantly, to having his longbow and arrows perfectly tuned. He knows exactly what his arrow will do, even before it leaves the bow.

This type of familiarity with your equipment comes with experience. You'll soon be able to notice any discrepancies in your own arrow flight and identify and correct the problem.

STRING SILENCERS

If you're a bowhunter, string silencers are a necessity to quiet the *twang* of the bowstring when you release the arrow. Game animals are attuned to the sounds around them and they're not used to hearing the hum of a bowstring.

There are several types of string silencers on the market, ranging from the Puff silencers made of yarn (the absolute worst) to silencers made of various types of hide and fur from animals such as beaver or musk ox. While these "fuzzy" animal-hide silencers do a good job of silencing, they also have the annoying propensity to pick up stick tights, beggar's lice, and every other weed seed with which they come into contact. When they get wet, every time you shoot an arrow you'll get a face full of spray. For my money, the rubber cat whisker silencers are the only way to go. They not only absorb the greatest amount of vibration, since they're made of rubber, but also shed weed seeds and other duff and provide the greatest amount of silencing with the least amount of performance loss. Keep in mind that any weight you add to the bowstring will slow the string down after the shot, albeit a very minimal amount.

Some longbow shooters who use cat whiskers will use a nocking point to secure them to the bowstring or serving material to tie them on. The method of attachment is up to you, but I simply tie them on using a plain old overhand knot, snugging them down very tightly. I've yet to have them come off, and I have several bows that have had the cat whisker silencers on them through several thousand shots with no sign of wear.

The key to getting the most silencing potential is to find the harmonic points on the upper and lower halves of your bowstring. Prior to putting on the silencers, grasp the bowstring at the point where the nocking point is located and "pluck" the upper portion of the bowstring, starting at the top and working your way down. You'll find a location on the string where the harmonic *twang* is the loudest—this is the point where the vibration is centered, and it's where you need to apply the silencer. Do the same for the lower half of the bowstring and you're all set.

Of course, traditional archery lends itself to experimentation and finding out what works best for the individual archer. Try different types of silencers to find which works best for you.

Installing string silencers on the bowstring will affect how your arrow flies. If you're going to use string silencers, install them before you begin the bare shaft tuning process.

NOCK ROTATION

Most longbow shooters I know, myself included, nock the arrow with the cock feather facing away from the bow. There are those who swear that they get better arrow flight with the cock feather pointed straight up. These shooters use only a small portion of rest material on the shelf and leave a gap between the shelf material and the strike plate on the riser. This forms a small gap and theoretically allows the bottom feather closest to the bow to pass over the shelf with minimum interference. I haven't tried this because I'm satisfied with my arrow flight, but if you feel like experimenting even further, you might give this a try.

FURTHER EXPERIMENTATION

Always remember that bows and arrows have individual personalities, just as we do. What works for one longbow shooter may not work for anyone else. As you gain experience and understanding of your longbow and learn to work with it, you'll discover different ways of tweaking your longbow to increase performance and accuracy. This may be something as simple as adjusting the height of the nocking point on the bowstring, padding the strike plate on the bow's riser, or adding thickness to the shelf rest on the arrow shelf. When you do things right, you'll see an improvement in arrow flight and accuracy. If your experiments don't work, hit the "undo" button and try something else. You'll eventually find just the right combination of everything to make your longbow's accuracy and efficiency almost effortless.

- 11 -

Advanced Accuracy
Exercises

Most people have seen well-known personalities such as Byron Ferguson performing trick shots with their longbows. Howard Hill was famous for these exhibitions, which he put on during the intermission of his famous movie, *Tembo*. Both are well known for shooting objects such as coins and cardboard discs out of the air. Hill once shot nine dimes in a row out of the air, and I've seen Ferguson shoot aspirin pills out of the air.

While these shots are truly amazing, they're far from impossible. Both Hill and Ferguson spent a great deal of time with their longbows, and that intimate familiarity taught them what their bows were capable of, if they did their part. I've duplicated a few of their feats myself, such as snuffing out the flame of a burning candle, shooting a playing card in two edgewise, and ricocheting an arrow off a sheet of plywood to burst a balloon. While these shots amaze crowds, the vast majority of audience members are either part-time archers, compound shooters, or have never shot a bow.

The truth of the matter is the longbow lends itself well not only to "trick shooting" but also to shooting from a variety of contorted positions you might encounter while hunting game. For instance, I can shoot my bow while laying flat on my stomach, turning backward, kneeling, squatting, laying on my back, and several other positions not normally thought about when shooting a longbow. Try doing that with a compound!

The longbow is a stable platform, and as long as you understand its capabilities and limitations, extreme and consistent accuracy can be achieved. As I've tried to emphasize throughout this book, proper

Scatter arrows randomly and then shoot each one from where it's located.

shooting form is essential to accuracy and consistency. The following exercises are designed both to give you faith in your ability to shoot the longbow and to help you develop your own practice regimen to further your abilities.

SCATTERED ARROWS

One of the keys to sharpening your instinctive eye and learning to judge what you need to do to make a shot is to move around and shoot at different distances and angles from the target. One of my favorite exercises—and one I practice every chance I get—is to scatter several arrows around the shooting range at different distances and angles from the target. I shoot each arrow from the spot where it lays. I may start out shooting an arrow from 10 yards, then move back to 25 yards, then up to 15, and then back to 20. By doing this, I don't get locked into shooting more than one arrow from the same distance. This exercise is extremely valuable for helping you to judge distances and how high you need to elevate your bow arm to get the arrow to the target.

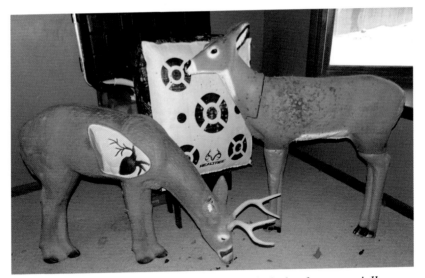

3D targets are excellent practice for hunting with the longbow, especially those that reflect the actual location of an animal's vital organs. By shooting at the target from different angles, you gain an understanding of what the arrow would have done on a live animal.

When shooting at a bag target or 3D animal targets (especially one that shows the actual location of the vital organs), it's always a good idea to practice shots from different angles. Notice that as the angle increases, the size of the kill zone decreases. What started out as a target area the size of a paper plate is now down to the width of your hand.

STUMP SHOOTING

If you've spent much time with a traditional bow in your hand, you've undoubtedly done some stump shooting. It's one of my favorite activities, and I've been known to frequently forego my pursuit of deer or turkeys in order to shoot stumps or other targets of opportunity with a blunt arrow.

I use one of two points for stump shooting. The first is the tried and true Zwickey Judo point, which consists of a flat point surrounded by four spring-loaded arms. This prevents the arrow from skipping or sliding under the grass or burying itself too far into a rotten stump. This point also makes an excellent small game head, and I've brought home many rabbits and squirrels that have fallen to a well-placed

My favorite stump-shooting heads are the Zwickey Judo point (left) and a .38-caliber casing glued over a field point (right).

Zwickey Judo point. The second is simply a .38-caliber cartridge casing glued over a field point. This head has a lot of shocking power and is also excellent for small game. I very seldom lose one while stump shooting.

The great thing about wandering through the woods and fields, picking targets to shoot at as you go, is that it helps your hand-eye coordination and muscle memory much more than shooting at a target in the backyard. Some of your shots while stump shooting may be uphill, downhill, or across a ravine. Any number of scenarios is possible, and each shot you take teaches you something. It's even more fun with a friend—one of you picks a target and the person whose arrow lands closest gets to choose the next one.

As your instinctive shooting skills grow, you'll find that you're able to make a shot without coming to anchor. You should still come to a full draw, but your instinctive abilities will develop to the point that you can feel where the shot will go. For example, I can shoot just as accurately by drawing the bow to my chest or out to the side of my face as I can when I come to solid anchor. This is simply because I have shot so many thousands of arrows that I *know* what my arrow will do. Is that to say that I never miss? Quite the opposite. I make some major-league misses, especially when it comes to the wild turkey. I've missed the same mature gobbler from a range of 10 feet, 20 feet, 25 feet, and a little farther. The fact is, I shot my whole quiver full of broadheads at that turkey and never touched a feather. I've killed caribou in Canada and every type of game animal in my home state of Indiana, except for the Eastern wild turkey. But I digress . . .

LONG-DISTANCE SHOOTING

If you're like me, you read every bowhunting magazine you can get your hands on, even in the "off season" (but there really is no off season for me). Many famous compound bow shooters often talk about shooting long-range targets—out to 100-plus yards—to fine-tune their shooting at targets within bowhunting range. All those who practice this technique swear by it. Those who do spot-and-stalk hunting in the western United States, where there is very little cover, are often faced with shots from distances of 40 to 60 yards. There simply is no other option.

As instinctive shooters, we don't have to worry about rangefinders or sight pins, but we can still benefit from increasing our effective range. The saying "Aim small, miss small" applies well here. In order for compound shooters to be effective at extreme yardages, their equipment must be tuned perfectly and their shooting form flawless. The same applies to instinctive shooting with the longbow. In order to successfully hit a target out past your normal distance, you must concentrate that much more and pay close attention to each facet of your shooting form. Close to the target, a small imperfection here or there won't affect accuracy that much. However, at longer distances even small inconsistencies will be magnified because the arrow is in flight for a longer period of time. What you thought was a perfectly tuned arrow at 20 yards may develop a bad nock left yaw at 40 or 50 yards because you squeezed the bow too hard and caused the string to torque. Uneven finger pressure on the bowstring can cause the back of the arrow to bounce off the arrow shelf instead of gliding smoothly over it. This may not make any difference when shooting at a whitetail from a tree stand at a distance of 12 yards, but you'll definitely see the effects if you do the same thing when shooting at a target at 50 yards.

Practice shooting at longer distances to further refine your shooting form and to fine-tune your equipment. Eventually you should see your maximum effective range increase a few yards and those shots at 20 yards or closer will be a "slam dunk."

By this point, your archery tackle should be as fine-tuned as possible, and your shooting skills should be improving with every practice session. Never let yourself be fooled into thinking you're as good as you're going to get. To the best of my knowledge, Hill and maybe Ferguson have reached the closest to perfection a human can come with a longbow. Never stand on your laurels and never stop challenging your-self with your longbow. Always look for a better way of doing things. I'm only human, the same as you, and what works for me may not work exactly for you. Don't be afraid to experiment, and keep striving for that perfect shot!

- 12 -

Hunting
with the Longbow

While there are plenty of longbow shooters who are content with target shooting, the vast majority of us are hunters. Some believe the urge to hunt is the result of an ancient gene left over from our ancestors, but no matter what the reason, it's a need that can only be satisfied by the act of actually being out there, pursuing whatever game is in season. There may be many legal weapons to engage in that pursuit, but for the longbow hunter there is only one tool that will suffice: a simple bent stick and string, with a quiver full of feathered missiles. Game taken any other way, while appreciated, never has the same meaning as game taken with the longbow, on the animal's own turf and giving the animal every advantage.

Hunting with the longbow is nothing like hunting with a shotgun, rifle, or compound bow. First, your shooting range is limited by your skill with your longbow, as well as by the animal's proximity. You also must take into account the animal's state of mind. Is it alert? Is it trying to get the scent of something it doesn't believe belongs there? Has it detected an intrusion? The only really acceptable shot on a game animal is if its head is obscured by a tree or brush and if it isn't on red alert. Shots at relaxed animals tend to negate their ability to "jump the string," or react to the sound of the bow shot. All game animals spend their lives constantly on the lookout for predators, especially around water holes or concentrated areas of food. Game animals realize that predators (other than us) understand that the easiest time for an ambush is while feeding.

To be a successful longbow hunter, you have to cover all your bases. You must hunt downwind of the animal's expected route of

approach and do everything within your power to control your scent. You also must disturb the natural habitat as little as possible. The best way to accomplish this is to have the best-possible understanding of your quarry's habits. Finally, you also must have adequate concealment or camouflage to cover your draw.

When I killed my biggest buck on November 18, 2013, the 140-class buck was within 20 yards of my blind for over an hour, and he and the accompanying does had no idea I was anywhere near. My success was a result of years of prior observation, knowledge of the white-tailed buck's habits during the rut, his habitat and core area, and more than a lion's share of patience. It was not only the most demanding hunt I've ever had, but also the most rewarding. Patience and the ability to make the right decision at the right time can only come with experience. This applies no matter what type of game you seek. Learn as much about them as you can—get to know their habits, their preferred areas, their bedrooms, and where they go to seek food and breeding opportunities.

WOODSMANSHIP

As with any type of hunting, whether with rifle, shotgun, or bow, woodsmanship is the key to success. Knowing your quarry and its habits and habitat very well is always the best place to start. This is true regardless of the species you're hunting, and these tips apply across the board. I read everything I can get my hands on, from scientific studies to hunting stories in magazines, to pick up any information or tactics I might not have been aware of before. I also familiarize myself with the area I'll be hunting as much as possible, even before I get there. Websites like TerraServer and Google Earth can provide you with satellite photos of your hunting area, helping you to eliminate unproductive ground and identify likely ambush locations at the same time. When coupled with a topographical map that shows changes in elevation, hilltops, valleys, and other major terrain features, you can get a good idea of what your hunting area looks like before ever setting foot there. Preseason and post-season scouting is irreplaceable when it comes to garnering knowledge of your chosen quarry. At these times of year, you don't need to worry about upsetting the delicate balance of your quarry's day-to-day activities. When the season ends, it's the best time to get out there and find out what the animals have been doing in places that you may not have even been aware of. Finding old rub lines, scrape lines, wallows, and prime breeding areas can add to your success next year.

HUNTING METHODS

Hunting with the longbow requires a different mindset than hunting with a compound bow, where shots may be taken out to 50 yards or even farther with a finely tuned compound equipped with sights and a release aid. For the average longbow hunter, 15 to 20 yards is average, with 30 yards pushing the envelope. In order to get that close to your quarry, you have to use every advantage possible to get within range.

Tree Stands

Many hunters enjoy hunting from elevated tree stands. I used one for many years before back problems and subsequent surgery made it safer for me to keep both feet on the ground. When choosing a tree stand, it's important to remember that your longbow can present its own set of problems, the least of which is limited effective shooting range. Tree stands with safety bars across the front are next to impossible to shoot from, as the lower limb of the longbow invariably connects with this bar and makes it difficult to come to full draw, much less make a shot. Stands with an open front lend themselves much better to shooting the longbow, but even then shooting at a steep downward angle can result in the lower limb striking the platform. You must take your shots with care, and it's always a good idea, whenever possible, to practice shooting from your tree stand at targets placed in various locations around the tree, just to see what you can and can't do with your longbow. While you can shoot a longbow accurately from a variety of positions, pushing a bad shot at an animal is never a good idea.

Ground Blinds

Some locations don't lend themselves to tree stands, either because there are no trees in range of a good ambush location or because there are no trees at all. One of my favorite spots on a farm I hunt was logged recently, leaving no trees standing that were big enough to support a tree stand even if I had wanted to hunt from one. There were, however, plenty of brush piles left behind by the loggers, which allowed me to construct several very good ground blinds.

There are numerous commercial ground blinds on the market but I have yet to find one that's roomy enough to allow shooting from multiple positions with my longbow. Besides, part of the allure of the longbow is its simplicity. I don't like having to carry much while I'm hunting and have always been able to put something together out of natural materials on hand. When constructing a ground blind from materials at hand, it's imperative that you choose a downwind location that will give you a shot within the limits of your comfortable range. I generally try to pick a spot that has a large tree to use as a backstop, which also gives me something to lean against while I'm waiting for game. I collect as many limbs as possible that have already fallen to the ground, because cutting too many saplings and brush in the area of your blind will tip off wary game animals to the fact that something has changed. Just as you would notice if your living room had been rearranged when you came home from work, game animals are intimately familiar with their surroundings. If I need to cut additional brush or saplings, I do so a good distance from the location of my blind.

Ground blinds, whether natural or man-made, put you on the ground with the game animals.

If necessary, you can also use burlap netting to complete your blind. Build the sides of the blind up high enough to conceal you from approaching game but make sure you leave gaps to shoot through that correspond to shooting lanes where you plan to take a shot.

With the limited range of your longbow, you must pay particular attention to detail when setting up these blinds. The key is to be able to come to full draw without giving away your position. There are very few longbow shooters who can hold a hunting-weight bow at full draw for a great length of time. This means you must time your draw at a point when the animal is looking the other way, or when its head is behind a tree or bush or its vision otherwise obscured.

As with any ambush location, it's also of paramount importance to take into consideration the direction of the prevailing winds, as well as the direction from which you think the game will appear. Ungulates possess keen senses of hearing and vision, but their sense of smell is what they count on the most to keep them out of danger.

Composure

Given the excitement that accompanies such a close encounter, keeping your cool is not an easy thing to do, no matter how many times you've had similar encounters. That's the fun of hunting with the longbow. There's nothing like being close enough to the animal to see the guard hairs on its chin or the steam of its breath. You might be close enough to watch as it grazes, completely unaware of your presence, or to be charged at close range by a wild boar, just managing to get an arrow into it seconds before it runs you down. Situations like this are brought on by the longbow, by the necessity of getting close to the game, and only add to the exhilaration of the hunt.

Stillhunting

Another method I employ while hunting with my longbow is stillhunting. Stillhunting differs from stalking because you move like a shadow through the fields and forests, trying to become part of your surroundings rather than standing out. Stalking takes place when you've spotted a game animal and are doing your best to get close enough for a longbow shot. For the record, for every stalk I've successfully conducted on a game animal, a hundred more have come unraveled long before I was within range, thanks to fickle winds or being caught in mid-stride by a sharp-eyed deer or caribou.

Stillhunting is more art than science, and it requires planning. Many new hunters mistakenly believe that the easiest and quickest way to find game is to follow game trails. The logic is sound, but since game animals travel on game trails, they're going to see you long before you see them—every time. It's much better to travel slowly on the downwind side of the trail, about a bowshot away. As with blind hunting, it's also imperative to know what the wind is doing. Even on the best days, it's a safe bet that for every animal you see, there are ten that smell you before you even get close. That's just the nature of the game, and the only thing you can do is try to use the wind in your favor.

In simplest terms, always hunt with the wind in your face, or at least quartering to. This might mean taking a long detour around your hunting area and coming in from a different side to take advantage of the wind. Dedicated longbow hunters learned long ago that there's no shortcutting the wind. It's also important to remember that the wind behaves a lot like running water, swirling around hills and making

Stalking any game animal is a challenge, and I spend many hours doing just that every season.

eddies in depressions. I carry a squeeze bottle of odorless powder that helps me determine exactly what the wind is doing. One squeeze produces a cloud of powder that I can follow downwind. Of course, where the breeze goes, my human scent goes with it.

While stillhunting, move slowly and silently. Leave anything shiny or noisy at home. If you must carry a cell phone, set it to silent mode. Soft-soled shoes are a great asset here as they allow you to feel sticks under your feet before you put your full weight on them and cause them to break. For every step you take, check your surroundings twice. Look for the twitch of an ear, a white patch of fur, the glint of an antler, or any other sign that game is near. Use your ears as much as your eyes. Keep an arrow nocked and your longbow ready for action. Many times, if you move quietly enough, you'll come upon a game animal that is completely unaware of your presence. If you spend enough time in the fields and forests, they will begin to feel like home. You'll find that small game animals like squirrels and birds begin to pay less attention to you, accepting you as part of the environment.

When hunting on the ground, 3D camouflage, offered by these a ghillie suits, is an invaluable aid in keeping hidden from sharp-eyed game animals.

CAMOUFLAGE

Camouflage clothing is more of a personal choice than a necessity. To my knowledge, the only game animal that can truly see color is the wild turkey (see the sidebar on page 128). I often think the myriad of camouflage patterns on the market is more to satisfy the hunter than the hunted. Prior to Jim Crumley's invention of the Trebark camouflage pattern, hunters took to the field in dark-colored wool pants and wool shirts in muted checks and plaids, or in old military surplus camouflage pants and jackets.

Game animals are champions at recognizing the human form, regardless of the latest and greatest camo pattern. You're shaped like a human being, regardless of what you wear. The key is to change your outline and break up your human form. While I still wear camouflage shirts and pants (though I can't even tell you who made them or what pattern they are), I also wear a one-piece coverall covered with hundreds of leafy shapes that break up my human outline. I've had animals of every sort wander past me without giving me a second glance, and I firmly believe that they didn't pay any attention to me because my human form was not recognizable. I have no doubt that had I been wearing regular camouflage clothing, the animals would have picked me out in an instant.

Another form-concealing garment that I own but have yet to try is a ghillie suit, much like the ones used by snipers in our armed forces. I have no doubt that it will be just as effective.

SCENT

The most serious detriment to the longbow hunter is our human scent. Because the longbow requires such close proximity to your quarry, scent is likely to give you away before anything else. That's why it's so vitally important to play the wind and have at least a rudimentary understanding of what it does. In the morning as the air warms, thermals rise. In hilly and mountainous terrain, the thermals carry our scent uphill along with them. In the evenings, the opposite occurs—as the wind cools, it carries our scent downhill.

One trick I frequently employ when hunting from a blind is placing a scent wick saturated with either doe or buck urine (for whitetails) at the exact location I want the animal to stop. I try to place these scent wicks behind a thick bush or a large tree so that the animal's head is behind cover, giving me the opportunity to draw undetected.

To fool most game animals, you have to fool their noses first. These products have all proven themselves in the field.

There are several lines of clothing on the market that claim to contain human scent to a point where it won't disturb game animals. I have no experience with these as they're rather expensive and I prefer to spend my money on archery tackle. I do use scent-killing laundry detergent and sprays that are supposed to kill the bacteria that cause human odor. I have enough experience with these products to believe that they do work, at least to some degree. My morning pre-hunt ritual consists of a shower with scent-free or scent-killing body wash, followed by a generous application of deodorant with the same properties, and ending with spraying bare skin with scent-killer spray prior to dressing in my hunting clothes. Once dressed, my hunting clothes receive another liberal dose of the scent-killer spray, as well as my boots, bows, arrows, fanny pack, and anything else I'll be carrying with me. Even if they have no effect at all, they add to my confidence, and sometimes that's better than anything else.

EQUIPPING FOR THE HUNT

The night before the hunt has a ritual of its own. I go through all of my bowhunting equipment, starting with my longbow. I check the bow from top to bottom, looking for any cracks and checking the glue lines

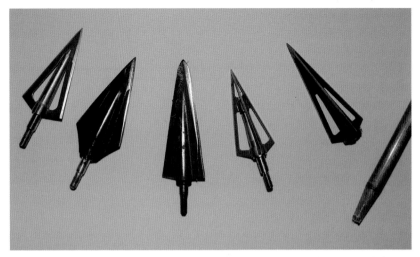

A razor-sharp broadhead that flies true is a requirement and a responsibility when you're hunting with the longbow. Anything less is both unethical and ineffective.

for integrity, along with the limb tips and nock grooves. Once I'm satisfied that my longbow is 100 percent, I check the bowstring for broken strands, then the nocking point and center serving to make sure neither has slipped out of position. I finish up the inspection with a fresh coat of bowstring wax, making sure to work it well into the strands.

Broadheads

I also perform a thorough arrow inspection, checking each one for cracks, damaged fletching, or loose broadheads. Once they all have passed inspection, I'll hone each broadhead with a file until it is shaving sharp. I recommend a quality two- or three-blade broadhead from a reputable manufacturer with a Rockwell hardness that makes the metal soft enough to sharpen easily but hard enough to hold an edge.

There is absolutely *no* excuse for going afield with anything less than shaving-sharp broadheads. As much as we hate to admit it, we all occasionally wound game by making a bad shot, and sometimes we fail to recover that animal. When this happens, I carry a sense of guilt for weeks, constantly replaying the shot in my mind and wondering if I could have done anything differently. I can live with the fact that I made a bad shot, but I would have a hard time forgiving myself if the errant

HUNTING THE WILD TURKEY

Don Thomas, co-editor of *Traditional Bowhunter* magazine, firmly believes that the wild turkey deserves a spot in the book of big game, and I heartily agree. After years of pursuing the Eastern wild turkey with my longbow and several embarrassingly close misses, I'm beginning to wonder what I'm doing wrong.

Wild turkeys have excellent hearing and remarkable vision. Luckily, their sense of smell is not a factor—if it were, we'd never get close enough to kill them. Their weakness is the fact that they're a gregarious lot, especially during the spring mating season, which is when most gobblers are taken. The sight of a mature gobbler spinning like a drunk in an effort to impress one or more hens would be comical if it weren't for the fact that they're so unpredictable. Turkeys are wired tightly and ready to panic at the drop of a hat. If they see you, they'll be more than willing to leave you all the property you want with no argument.

On the other hand, I've had jakes wander around within 10 yards of me, clucking and purring as though they had not a care in the world. Of course, this was several days after the season closed. I could've killed any one of 'em with a rock . . .

Killing a wild turkey requires a combination of being in the right place at the right time, sufficient camouflage, adequate concealment, and at least a rudimentary knowledge of turkey calls and the ability to reproduce them in a believable-enough manner to fool one of the birds into bow range. It occurs to me occasionally that killing a turkey with a longbow takes on the aura of a stunt as opposed to a real hunting goal.

The kill zone on a wild turkey is exceedingly small, roughly the size of a baseball, and the most widely accepted target is the wing butt. Another less aesthetically pleasing—yet highly effective—target is located at the south end of the turkey, just below the tail fan. An arrow through that small circle is sure to take out everything important as it

shot were the result of cheap or substandard equipment. Save yourself the heartache and invest in the best arrows and broadheads you can afford. Practice with them until you're as confident launching a broadhead from your longbow as you are when shooting field points. In my opinion, expandable broadheads have no place in bow hunting

HUNTING THE WILD TURKEY

passes through the boiler room. And, for those who are exceptional shots, the base of the neck is also a viable target. Another alternative is an arrow through the hips. While it won't be instantly fatal, it will prevent the turkey from building up enough speed to fly off and lose you.

The commonly accepted method of killing turkeys with a longbow centers around finding where the turkeys roost, then sneaking back in well before daylight and setting up some kind of blind on the edge of the field where the turkeys fly down. Of course, they're just as likely to fly down in the other direction, reducing all of your meticulous planning to naught, but a few carefully placed decoys can help convince the roosted turkeys that this is where they want to be.

Once the turkeys have spotted your decoys, call only often enough to keep their interest and do so softly, with occasional clucks and purrs. Once you have a turkey in bow range, try to wait until its attention is focused on a decoy or its head is hidden by the tail fan before you come to full draw. Having a fully enclosed blind with a darkened interior helps immensely. I don't have one, so I have to settle for whatever I can cobble together at the spur of the moment.

I don't know why turkeys rattle me so much when other longbow hunters take them routinely. I've missed turkeys at distances measured in feet and have even emptied a quiver at the same turkey, which never moved more than 10 yards away as he tried to figure out what the strange creature was hiding behind the bush. I eventually attempted to chase him down and grab him by the neck, an exercise which proved fruitless.

Of all the animals I've chased over the years with my longbow, I have to give the wild turkey first place as far as run-and-gun, interactive hunting goes. Some of my most cherished memories are not of turkeys I've taken, but rather of the sound of a quicksilver gobble on the edge of pink light, setting the tone for the morning with the knowledge that my quarry is indeed there, and that he might actually want to play the game.

and most definitely not on the end of an arrow being shot from a longbow.

If the weather is damp, I'll coat the cutting edge of each broadhead with a thin layer of petroleum jelly to prevent oxidation. Believe it or not, broadheads dull from exposure to nothing more than air.

Accessories

In addition to the obvious things you need to bow hunt, there are a few others items that come in handy. The following list is posted on the door of my gun cabinet. At the beginning of each season, I lay everything out and check it off as I pack it.

- **Daypack, fanny pack, backpack, or meat-carrying pack.** While most hunting clothes available today have pockets everywhere, I find it much easier to carry most of my gear in a daypack or fanny pack so I don't have to dig through my pockets.
- **Two knives.** I always carry a spare knife in case I lose one or break a blade. Whether folding or fixed-blade, a knife is one of those items that is irreplaceable when you need it. I once forgot to bring one and ended up having to field dress a whitetail with a broadhead.
- **Medium-cut bastard file (for broadheads) and a medium-grit sharpening stone (for knives).** A short 6- to 8-inch file is plenty for touching up broadheads in the field, and the sharpening stone keeps your knives ready to go. Believe it or not, a dull blade is just as dangerous as a sharp one because more force is needed to cut, increasing the chance of injury.
- **Game calls.** Carry a variety of game calls for deer, elk, or turkey season.
- **Gloves.** I carry several pairs of shoulder-length field dressing gloves and the same number of latex gloves. The shoulder-length gloves keep my sleeves clean when I'm field dressing game animals, and the rubber latex gloves help hold the field dressing gloves in place.
- **Point-and-shoot camera with a 6-inch tripod.** More often than not I hunt alone, and the self-timer feature and short tripod make those hero pictures a lot easier to take. I keep the camera in a shirt pocket in case an interesting subject comes along and I want to snap a few photos.
- **Hunting licenses.** This should be a no-brainer but I have been known to forget my tags at home.
- **Map and compass.** These are especially important when hunting in the big woods. Handheld GPS units are nice but don't always work when you want them to. I *highly* recommend carrying a topographical map of the area you're hunting and a

quality lensatic compass. If you don't know how to read and navigate using these items, do yourself a favor and take an orienteering class.

- **Binoculars.** These are optional if you're hunting in thick woods, but in wide-open areas a good set of binoculars can be invaluable in spotting game.
- **Fully charged cellular or satellite phone.** Many may disagree with me on this, but in case of an emergency sometimes a little technology is necessary even for us longbow hunters. Even if you carry a phone, always make sure someone knows *where and when* you're hunting and what time you should be home or back at camp.
- **A small survival kit.** My kit contains basic medical supplies, matches *and* a lighter, a space blanket, and a couple of small candles to use as fire starters.
- **Spare tackle.** Never go afield without at least one spare bowstring that has already been "shot in"; a spare shooting glove or tab; and a spare shelf rest or strike plate material. As my old SWAT instructor used to say, "It's better to have it and not need it, than to need it and not have it!"

This may seem like a lot of gear to carry, but everything I've listed above fits neatly in a medium-sized fanny pack or daypack and may end up being just what you need!

- 13 -

Care
and
Maintenance

Just like your vehicle, your longbow and arrows require regular care and maintenance. Worn bowstrings and cracked or bent arrows can break, causing catastrophic damage to your bow and putting you at risk of injury. I take the time to look over my longbow every day before I shoot, checking to make sure there are no cracks, that none of the laminations have separated, and that the string nocks are in good shape.

BOWSTRING

If the bowstring has any broken strands, I replace it immediately. When putting on a new string, I always leave it strung on the bow overnight to get as much stretch out as possible before setting the brace height and shooting it. Even with new string materials like Fast Flight, there is still a small amount of stretching that takes place as the string wax gets squeezed out of the strands.

If the string starts to appear fuzzy, it's time to apply bowstring wax. String wax protects and lubricates the strands against the friction that takes place when drawing and shooting the bow. Keeping your strings waxed regularly will help them last a lot longer.

Once I've given the bow and string a good once-over, I string the bow and gently draw it a few times, listening for any creaks, groans, or popping noises that might indicate some internal problem. Takedown longbows are more prone to making noises than one-piece longbows, and you should take extra care to make sure that all attachment points are tight and serviceable. A little lubricant in the form of bowstring wax will take care of any normal squeaks.

A well-waxed bowstring will last a lot longer because the individual strands stay lubricated and the wax reduces the friction between them. Wax will also help with the fuzziness that results as tiny fibers break over time from wear and tear on the string.

ARROWS

Next, I move on to my arrows. While I shoot both wood and carbon arrows, there is still a large number of archers who shoot aluminum arrows. Regardless of what type you shoot, a bent or crooked arrow will not fly straight, so you need to check them for straightness. A tool on the market called a spin tester consists of a platform with ball bearing rollers at each end. By placing the arrow on these rollers and spinning it, any imperfection becomes immediately obvious. I'm a bit lower tech and simply place my arrows on a cutting board, allowing the fletching and point ends to extend over the edges so the arrow can roll freely. By rolling the arrow back and forth on the cutting board, I can easily notice any problems.

As mentioned earlier, wood arrows take a bit more TLC than carbon or aluminum arrows since they can "wander." No matter how well they're sealed, they can still draw moisture and warp. Straightening wood arrows is a science in itself and one, I must confess, that I've never quite mastered. I've generally been able to get by with the

PROTECTING THE WOOD IN YOUR BOWS AND ARROWS

Most longbows contain at least some wood, and as everyone knows, wood and moisture don't get along well. Water can make wood swell and deteriorate. This is precisely why bowyers use multiple layers of finish on their bows. I once owned a cheap off-the-shelf longbow on which the sides of the limbs were not sanded smooth or finished properly. While hunting during wet weather, I could see the moisture soaking into the wood laminations under the fiberglass backing on my bow. When I got home, I unstrung the bow and hung it up to dry. Four hours later, I heard a loud *crack* and found that the moisture absorbed by the wood laminations between the fiberglass laminations had swollen to the point that both limbs delaminated.

Longbows are also going to get dings and nicks. Some of these are minor, but some can cause just enough of a break in the finish to allow moisture to seep in. When you finish hunting for the day, look your longbow over again from top to bottom, checking for nicks or gouges that got into the wood or between the wood laminations and fiberglass laminations. If you find any dings like this, the best thing to do is use superglue (cyanoacrylate) to seal the nick or gouge and keep out the water.

judicious application of low heat and a gentle but constant bend in the opposite direction of the warped section. If anything more is required, I usually relegate that shaft to the woodpile. Fortunately, with the availability of modern sealants and dips, warped shafts have become more the exception than the rule. Aluminum arrows, on the other hand, are impossible to straighten once they're bent. It's best just to relegate them to the garden to serve as tomato stakes. There are tools available to help take slight bends out of aluminum arrows, but I'm not sure how well they work.

Carbon arrows—my favorite, even though they're not "traditional" to most hardcore traditionalists—are either straight or broken. No amount of bending affects their straightness. To check their integrity, all I do is give them a gentle bend, followed by a twist. If you hear a cracking noise during either test, then the carbon fibers in the shaft have been compromised and the shaft is no longer safe to shoot. Carbon arrows can definitely take a pounding and come out the other side ready to shoot again.

Superglue is perfect for sealing scratches, nicks, and dings in your longbow.

Feather fletching is the most common type of steering system on arrows for longbows since it's flexible and tends to fold down as it passes over the arrow shelf. The fletching can get a bit bedraggled from frequent shooting and passing through targets. This condition doesn't cause any problems for target shooting, but it does tend to be noisy in flight, which can be a detriment when hunting. The only time I shoot my hunting arrows is to check their flight with broadheads. Otherwise, they stay in the quiver and are used solely for hunting.

The last thing I do prior to shooting my arrows is spin them on the field point or broadhead to make sure the point or broadhead is sitting squarely on the arrow. A bent point or broadhead will rob the arrow of accuracy and, with a broadhead, may cause the arrow to fly wildly off at a tangent. If I can't get a broadhead on a hunting arrow to spin true, I replace it immediately with one that does. If you have problems with your points coming loose, try applying a little bowstring wax to the threads. This will usually solve the problem.

OTHER COMPONENTS

I always use a bow tip protector over the lower limb tip on all my bows. We all have a tendency to rest our longbows on the bottom tip when standing still, glassing for game, or resting our bow against a tree. Unprotected, the limb tip can gradually wear away, be exposed to moisture, and affect the glue bond in the tip overlays. The tip protector also protects the lower string loop and string grooves. It's a cheap solution to a potentially serious problem.

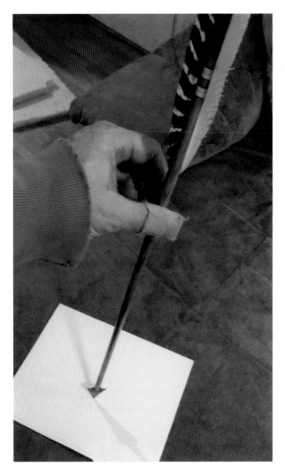

Spin testing your broadheads prior to hunting will help ensure accuracy.

Always check the shelf rest and strike plate material for excessive wear or for dirt or other matter than can make game-spooking noise when you draw your bow. Shelf rests and strike plates should last many years and be replaced if the adhesive is worn off to the point where they are coming loose from the bow. It's also possible, if you shoot as much as I do, to wear a hole through the shelf rest. This is a no-brainer and gets replaced immediately.

Shooting gloves and arm guards can also deteriorate. Sweat and natural oils from the body can cause stitching to weaken and leather to break down. This is unavoidable, and for that reason I always carry an extra shooting glove just in case my main glove decides to go south.

STORAGE

I always unstring my longbows when I'm finished shooting them and store them lying across on a pair of brackets mounted about 24 inches apart on the wall. You can also hang your bows from a peg by the upper string loop.

Never leave your longbow standing up on either limb, as this can eventually cause damage to the limb. Also avoid storing your longbow or arrows in a hot vehicle or any area where high temperatures are a factor.

Your longbow and tackle will last you many enjoyable years if you pay attention to your gear. A little time and effort on a regular basis can save you the expense of a new bow, or worse yet a trip to the emergency room. Pay attention to the details and never take anything for granted.

Resources

PUBLICATIONS
Traditional Bowhunter **magazine**
    PO Box 519
    Eagle, ID 83616
    (888) 828-4882; www.tradbow.com

Traditional Bowhunter magazine is one of the best sources for information and books pertaining to the longbow. Multitudes of bowyer advertisements are contained within its pages, and every bowyer listed will most likely be happy to answer any questions you may have about longbows and traditional archery in general.

Primitive Archer **magazine**
    PO Box 79306
    Houston, TX 77279
    (713) 467-8202; www.primitivearcher.com

Primitive Archer magazine is dedicated to the selfbow enthusiast and features how-to articles for making selfbows, as well as hunting stories and resource information for primitive archery supplies.

TRADITIONAL ARCHERY SUPPLIERS
Keep in mind that there are literally hundreds of traditional archery suppliers and traditional bowyers who make fine longbows. I've only listed the ones here that I've had personal experience with. Looking

through the pages of *Traditional Bowhunter* or searching the internet will undoubtedly provide more information than I can here.

3Rivers Archery

607 H. L. Thompson Jr. Dr.
PO Box 517
Ashley, IN 46705
(866) 587-9501; www.3RiversArchery.com

3Rivers Archery is a premier supplier of all things related to traditional archery. They have their own line of longbows, along with a complete line of traditional archery gear, including arrows of all types. The courteous and knowledgeable staff is more than happy to answer any questions you may have. They frequently get my business, and I have nothing but high marks for this company.

Kustom King Traditional Archery

5435 W. 75th Ave.
Schererville, IN 46375
(877) LONGBOW (566-4269); www.kustomkingarchery.com

Kustom King Archery is another major traditional archery supplier and one that I've done frequent and highly satisfactory business with in the past.

Rose City Archery

94931 Quiet Valley Ln.
PO Box 5
Myrtle Point, OR 97458
(866) 762-2776; www.rosecityarchery.com

Rose City Archery is a supplier of premium wood shafting, finished arrows, bows, and other tackle. One of the nation's oldest traditional archery suppliers, Rose City Archery provides everything needed to make your own arrows.

Alaska Bowhunting Supply
(Warehouse and Distribution Center)
3420 38th Ave. West
Seattle, WA 98199
(206) 453-3821; www.alaskabowhunting.com

Alaska Bowhunting Supply was one of the first companies to begin producing carbon arrows. Their GrizzlyStik carbon arrow comes in three different models, plus a parallel version, for a variety of draw weights.

CUSTOM BOWYERS

I have had the pleasure of meeting and speaking with a number of custom bowyers over the years and had the privilege of handling and shooting many fine longbows. Bowyers' pride in their workmanship is evident, and their reward is seeing the faces of those who handle and shoot their bows. Their true payment is the satisfaction of a job well done and hearing customers say, "That's exactly what I was looking for. Thank you."

Fox Archery
Ron King
701 W. Hwy 82
Wallowa, OR 97885
(541) 886-9110; www.foxarchery.com

I've owned three of Ron's fantastic longbows and have no reservations about recommending his work. Ron's longbows have accounted for a great many animals and a lot of meat in my freezer. His attention to fit and finish are impeccable, and his bows have to be seen to be appreciated!

TimberHawk Bows
> Scott Mitchell
> 7895 S. State Rd. 446
> Bloomington, IN 47401
> (812) 837-9340; www.timberhawkbows.com

I own one of Scott's phenomenal Falcon longbows, which I used to take down the biggest buck of my career during the fall of 2013. Scott's ability to blend wood and glass into a functional work of art is nothing short of amazing. I highly recommend his bows.

Black Widow Bows
> 1201 Eaglecrest St.
> PO Box 2100
> Nixa, MO 65714
> (417) 725-3113; www.blackwidowbows.com

I've owned three Black Widow bows—two longbows and a recurve—and have nothing but praise for the workmanship. In 2001, I took a huge bull caribou in the Northwest Territories during a very difficult hunt in high winds. My Ironwood longbow came through when I needed it to.

BOOKS
Barker, Juliet. *Agincourt: Henry V and the Battle that Made England*. New York: Back Bay Books/Little, Brown and Co., 2007.

Featherstone, Donald. *The Bowmen of England: The Story of the English Longbow*. New York: C. N. Potter, 1968.

———. *History of the English Longbow*. New York: Dorset Press, 1993.

Goodwin, George. *Fatal Colours: Towton 1461—England's Most Brutal Battle*. New York: W. W. Norton & Company, 2012.

Hill, Howard. *Hunting the Hard Way*. Lanham, MD: Derrydale Press, 2000.

———. *Wild Adventure*. Lanham, MD: Derrydale Press, 2000.

Pope, Saxton. *Hunting with the Bow and Arrow*. San Francisco, CA: The James H. Barry Co., c. 1923. (Reprints available from 3Rivers Archery, Kustom King Archery, Amazon, and several other booksellers.)

Thomas, E. Donnall Jr. *Longbows in the Far North: An Archer's Adventures in Alaska and Siberia*. Mechanicsburg, PA: Stackpole Books, 2007.

Glossary

Archer's paradox. Archer's paradox occurs when the arrow flexes around the riser when launched. All arrows flex when the bowstring is released and the string pushes on the back of the arrow, but the amount of flex is important because it determines how well the arrow flies (too stiff or not stiff enough).

Arrow rest. Also *arrow shelf*. A small piece of wood or leather glued to the side of the bow on which the arrow sits while drawing and shooting.

Bad release. A bad release occurs when the archer fails to release the bowstring cleanly.

Bow square. A tool shaped like the letter T with scale markings that allow the archer to measure both the brace height and nock location on the bowstring.

Bowyer. A bow maker.

Brace height. Also *fistmele*; the distance from the bowstring to the innermost portion of the inside of the grip.

Center serving. The location on the bowstring where the arrow snaps on and the archer grasps the string to draw the bow.

Deflex. The bow limbs sweep gently back toward the archer.

Delamination. Delamination occurs when the adhesive holding the different veneers or fiberglass strips together fails and the veneers and lamination come apart.

Draw check bow. A very light draw weight bow with a permanently attached arrow marked with a scale in inches; used to measure an archer's draw length.

Draw length. The measurement from the inside of the groove on the arrow nock to the point where the arrow passes over the far side of the arrow shelf.

Draw weight. Draw weight is the amount of force, measured in pounds, required to draw the bow to the industry standard of 28 inches. Custom bows can be ordered with a specific draw weight at the archer's draw length.

Endless loop strings. This type of bowstring is manufactured from a single strand of string material that is wound in a loop until there are sufficient strands to withstand a particular draw weight. The end loops that go on the ends of the bow limbs are fashioned by pulling the endless loop into a single strand, with the serving smaller loops at each end.

Flatbow. A shorter longbow that has wide, thin limbs similar to those of a recurve bow.

Flemish strings. These are created using separate bundles of string material, the ends of which are braided together to form loops. The string loops at each end are held together by twisting the bowstring. If a Flemish string is untwisted too much, it will come apart.

Fletching. Fletching is the term used to describe either feathers that have already been attached to the arrow, or the actual act of gluing the feathers onto the arrow. Feather fletching comes in different shapes and lengths. Parabolic feathers are rounded at the back, "banana"-cut feathers are higher in the middle than at either end, and shield-cut feathers are like parabolic feathers but with a slight dish-shaped cutout at the back end.

Flu-flu. Untrimmed feathers, typically 6 to 8 inches long, spiraled around the upper end of an arrow to slow it down and make it easier to locate.

Gap shooting. Using the point of the arrow as an aiming device, in conjunction with known distances, much like using sight pins on a compound bow.

Lamination. A thin strip of wood or fiberglass used in the construction of a laminated longbow.

Locator grip. A slight depression in the grip that allows the archer to grip the bow in the same spot each time for consistency between shots.

Longbow. A bow made of wood or wood and fiberglass laminations on which the bowstring touches only the string nocks at each end of the bow.

Maximum effective range. The farthest distance at which you can consistently shoot five out of six arrows into a paper plate.

Off-the-shelf shooting. Shooting an arrow directly off of the arrow shelf, without the use of any mechanical or elevated rest.

Point of aim. The distance where the point of the arrow is placed directly over the intended point of impact.

Recurve. A traditional bow with sweeping curves in the upper and lower limbs, easily identified by the fact that the bowstring contacts the limbs at the apex of the curve on both limbs.

Reflex. The bow limbs sweep away from the archer toward the front of the bow.

Riser. The vertical section of the bow that is above the arrow shelf.

Selfbow. A longbow carved from a single piece of wood, with no fiberglass lamination.

Shelf depth. The distance the shelf is cut from the center of the bow; used to determine arrow spine and how close the arrow lies to the center of the bow.

String grooves. Also *string nocks* or *nock grooves;* grooves cut into the limp tips to hold the string in place.

Tillering. The process of ensuring the upper and lower limbs of the bow work smoothly and equally throughout the draw.

Tip overlay. Extra material glued over limb tips for added strength.

Index

Page numbers in italics indicates illustrations and sidebars.